UNHURRIED
Time With GOD

UNHURRIED
Time With GOD

Jeff Wells

PUBLISHING CO.

Published in Austin, Texas, by JPM Publishing Co. Publisher can be reached at jpmpublishingco@gmail.com or via the contact form at www.jpmpublishingco.com.

Ordering Information:
Quantity sales. Special discounts are available on quantity purchases by corporations, associations, and others. For details, contact the publisher at the address above.

ISBN: 978-1-7332291-3-5 (Paperback)

Library of Congress Control Number: 2019917939

Printed in the United States of America

JPM Publishing Co.
www.jpmpublishingco.com

For the wonderful congregation I serve Jesus with at WoodsEdge Church – elders team, staff team and people. Gayle and I love you so much!

Contents

Foreword

In his new book, Unhurried Time With God, Jeff Wells addresses the vital spiritual strategy that every Christian must know and practice. The Apostle Paul tell us in Ephesians 6:10 that we are to "Be strong in the Lord and in the power of His might." This command was given in the context of spiritual warfare that all believers encounter on a daily basis. Obviously, not all Christians are strong or the instruction would be meaningless.

But the important question is, how can we be strong IN the Lord if we are not WITH the Lord daily? The occasional quoting of scripture and claiming our position in Christ will never do away with the necessity of spending time with Jesus. The lives of all spiritually strong Christian men and women throughout history prove this point.

Pastor Wells gives valuable instructions and examples of how time with God can become a daily habit for all of us. Read this book with an open heart and an ear tuned to the Holy Spirit.

Pastor Jim Cymbala
The Brooklyn Tabernacle

Chapter One

MY JOURNEY

It was the fall of 1972. I was a freshman at Rice University in Houston and a new Christian. I was excited about my new faith in Jesus and hungry to learn more.

During the Christmas break, my roommate, John Lodwick, and I went to a conference in Dallas, where 3,000 college students had gathered to learn more about Christ.

The speaker was Howard Hendricks, a professor at Dallas Theological Seminary and a powerful speaker. He would speak each morning, and at one point he challenged us: "If you are serious about knowing God, then you will decide to meet with God every day for prayer and Bible study."

When I heard that challenge, immediately my heart leapt within me. I thought: "Yes! I want that! I want to know God deeply! I am going to start doing this: Every day, I'll take time alone with God for prayer and Bible study."

When John and I returned to Rice to start the spring semester, we each began doing this, meeting with God daily for prayer and Bible study. We were distance runners on the Rice track team and we would get up early to run six miles around campus. Then we'd eat a large breakfast and go find a place on the campus to get this time alone with God before class.

I found a place in the large basement of my dorm. The room was filled with old furniture and rolled up carpets. It was dark and dusty, but I was alone and uninterrupted and this became my special place to meet with God. I would spend a half-hour praying and reading in the Bible, jotting notes in a blue spiral notebook.

This time with God became part of my daily life. There were no lightning bolts or dramatic encounters, but I would show up day after day to draw close to God. I was learning how to pray by praying, and I was discovering truth from the Bible. My relationship with God became more personal – first hand, rather than by proxy.

Nearly 50 years later, this time is still a huge part of my life. More so than ever. This time with God is commonly called a quiet time. However, sometimes the time is not quiet! There can be singing and loud praying and lamenting. For me, it is never completely quiet. I much prefer to pray out loud, and sometimes quite loudly! Perhaps a better term for it would be meeting with God, or time alone with God, or unhurried time with God. This time has morphed over the years. In some ways, it's always changing. I continually tweak how I approach this time with God, exactly what I do and how long I do it.

On a number of occasions I have read through the entire Bible, Genesis to Revelation. At other times I have read through the One Year Bible, which means you read through the Bible in a year, with a selection each day from the Old Testament, the New Testament, the Psalms and Proverbs. At other times, I have made my way through individual books in the Bible, taking a few weeks or a month.

For some years now, my strong preference has been to be reading in two or three places at once, say from the Old Testament, from one of the Gospels, and one of Paul's letters. But I do not try to get through a certain number of verses each day. Rather, I will prayerfully meditate in the passage until it seems like I am done. It might be a couple of chapters in the Old Testament or it might be a couple of verses in the New Testament – however far I get.

In a similar way, my praying has also changed over the years – how much worship and thanksgiving, how much singing, how I approach petition and intercession. In recent years I have done more listening, asking God to speak to me and jotting down things I believe God is putting on my heart.

When I began this journey I would sit in a folding metal chair for the half hour. Some years later I realized that I don't enjoy sitting still in a chair and so now I spend most of the time on my feet, slowly walking as I read and sing and pray.

These days I spend a lot more time with God than I used to, but I enjoy it a lot more. It is less duty and discipline and more delight. What's important to me is that I connect with God, that I draw close to God, that I meet with God. Also, I want the time to be unhurried. It is difficult to love anyone, including God, if you are hurrying.

However let me mention, even if you meet with God for prayer and Bible study out of duty and discipline, God will use it. Down deep, you want to know God and love God more, and God will meet with you and use this time in your life. Be encouraged.

For some years now, this daily meeting with God has become invaluable to me. It's rich and personal, free and loving. I'm still learning how to make this time with God more and more meaningful, but it has become the favorite part of my day. *I love it!* This is the time I get alone with my God and my Savior, with the Lover of my soul. There is nothing like it and I look forward to it each morning. I enjoy it thoroughly and I could not survive without it.

John White was a British writer and medical doctor. At times he was also a missionary and pastor. I loved his writings. In one book he wrote passionately about how much the Bible had meant to him.

> In the darkest periods of my life when everything seemed hopeless, I would struggle in the grey dawns of many faraway countries to grasp the basic truths of Scripture passages. I looked for no immediate answers to my problems. Only did I sense intuitively that I was drinking drafts from a fountain that gave life to my soul.
>
> Slowly as I grappled with textual and theological problems, a strength grew deep within me. Foundations cemented themselves to an other-worldly rock beyond the reach of time and space, and I became strong and more alive. If I could write poetry about it I would. If I could sing through paper, I would flood your soul with the glorious melodies that express what I have found. I cannot exaggerate for there are no expressions majestic enough to tell of the glory I have seen or of the wonder of finding that I, a neurotic, unstable, middle-aged man have my feet firmly planted in eternity and breathe the air of heaven. And all this has come to me through a careful study of Scripture. (*The Fight*, 54-55)

Oh I so identify with White! That's exactly how I have felt about this daily time alone with my God. It has meant more to me than I could possibly express.

The Catholic priest and writer, Thomas Merton, puts it more succinctly, but he is equally passionate.

> By the reading of Scripture I am so renewed that all nature seems renewed … The whole world is charged with the glory of God and I feel fire and music under my feet.

Merton's statement is so powerful! I know exactly what he means.

It has now been 42 years since I heard the challenge from Howard Hendricks. This time in the secret place, alone and unhurried, has become the foundation and the rock of my life. It has become the fire and music under my feet. It has become *the* privilege of my life.

PURPOSE OF THE BOOK

This is my purpose in writing: To urge you to meet with God. Alone. Each day. In an unhurried time of prayer and Bible reading. This is not a time of religious duty or checking a box to be spiritual. This is a time to meet with God. To draw close. To love and be loved.

This book is broken into four parts. Part I discusses the main reasons for meeting with God and addresses why, despite all of those reasons, we maintain a strange reluctance to do so.

Part II provides some practical guidelines for how we can overcome this "strange reluctance".

Part III dives deeper into what your time can look like as you meet with God. It's important to note that this secret place – the place where you connect with the God in Heaven – is a personal space. There is no one way this should look, no one method better than others.

Part IV wraps up with my responses to common questions and push-back I have received over the years on this topic.

In these next chapters, I outline the main reasons why this time alone with God means so much to me.

Firstly, I want to love God more. This will not happen unless I spent gobs of unhurried time alone with him. A.W. Tozer once wrote, "God doesn't have favorites but he does have intimates." I want to be one of God's intimates.

Secondly, I need this time. I need it for my sanity. For my emotional and spiritual health. For restoring my soul. I need it so I don't burn out and wither away. I need this time.

Thirdly, I want this time. I desire to meet with God. Over the years, God has given me a thirst for him, a longing for him. I enjoy this time. If I didn't do this each day, I'd miss him.

Fourthly, God wants this time. He desires for me to meet with him. I want this time, but God also wants it. He's my Father and he loves me dearly. Of course he wants me to come to him each day and draw close. What loving father wouldn't want to spend time alone with a much-loved child!

Each one of these reasons, by itself, is reason enough to make this time with God a daily priority. Together these reasons are especially compelling.

PART I

REASONS AND RELUCTANCE
FOR TIME WITH GOD

CHAPTER TWO

I WANT TO LOVE GOD MORE

———

First of all, I make this time alone with God a priority in my life because I want to love God more and know God better. I want to be one of God's intimates.

For this first reason, two passages loom large for me, two of the great passages in the Bible: Jeremiah 9:23-24 on knowing God and Matthew 22:34-38 on loving God. We will consider each of these passages in turn. First is Jeremiah 9:23-24.

> Thus says the LORD: "Let not the wise man boast in his wisdom, let not the mighty man boast in his might, let not the rich man boast in his riches, but let him who boasts boast in this, that he understands and knows me, that I am the LORD who practices steadfast love, justice, and righteousness in the earth. For in these things I delight, declares the LORD."

God names three things that were of supreme importance to the people of Jeremiah's day – wisdom, might and riches. Not surprisingly, these three things are supremely important to the people of our day also. To use slightly different words, these three values are education, the body, and money. These are probably the three greatest values in our culture.

God has a message for us, just as he had a message for the people of Jeremiah's day: "Don't boast about these things. Don't glory in them. Don't be enamored with them."

This does not mean that wisdom, might and riches are bad things. They are not. They are good things. Just do not live for them, because when you live for them, when you glory in them, they become bad things. They become idols. This is the point of the first commandment. *"You shall have no other gods before me" (Exodus 20:3).* Any time we put something before God, that thing becomes an idol.

Consider our culture: Is learning important to us? Degrees? Getting good grades and getting into the right college? For the typical parent in America, these things take on paramount importance.

Or take the body and everything that goes with it – athletic prowess, fitness and appearance, hair and make-up, nutrition and diets, plastic surgery. How much attention do we in the United States give to these things? How many billions do we spend, *on each one of these?* Understand, I love to run. I love sports. I'm glad that Gayle, my wife, wears make-up and wants to look beautiful for me (which she is of course, both with and without make-up). But these things can become all-important. When a good thing becomes the main thing, then that is a bad thing.

And then there's money, the biggest value of all in our culture. Salary, income, retirement, financial security, houses, cars, clothes, our toys – money and the things money can buy. Again, it is not that money is evil. Money is not even the root of evil. The love of money *is* the root of evil, and it is pervasive in our culture.

God puts his finger on the three biggest values of Jeremiah's day and the three biggest values of our day, and says to every one of us: *"Don't live for these things. Don't glory in these things. Don't let them become all-important to you."*

So what *do* we live for? What do we glory in? What must become all-important to us?

Knowing God. *"But let him who boasts boast in this, that he understands and knows me" (Jeremiah 9:24, emphasis added).*

This is not knowing *about* God. This is knowing *God*. Knowing God personally, intimately, lovingly. This is not merely head knowledge. It's also heart knowledge. So many people know *about* God. They fill our churches. Far fewer people *know* God himself. That is, they know God's character, God's ways,

God's voice, God's heart. They *know* God! They are intimates of God.

Augustine was one of those intimates. He once wrote, "Give me [your own] self, without whom, though [you should] give me all that [you have ever] made, yet [my desires could not be satisfied]." Augustine did not want wisdom, might and riches. He wanted God!

When I was a freshman in college and a new Christian, a senior on the track team, John Powell, gave me a book to read. The book was *Knowing God* by J.I. Packer. John chose wisely. The book was new at the time, but over the next 50 years it became a modern Christian classic.

These lines in the book captured my heart:

> What were we made for? To know God. What aim should we set ourselves in life? To know God. What is the 'eternal life' that Jesus gives? Knowledge of God. 'This is life eternal, that they might know thee, the only true God, and Jesus Christ, whom thou hast sent' (John 17:3). What is the best thing in life, bringing more joy, delight, and contentment, than anything else? Knowledge of God. (*Knowing God*, p. 29)

Reading these words was like listening to Howard Hendricks's challenge at the Christmas conference. My heart resonated deeply with Packer's call and I thought: "Yes! That's what I want! I want to know God that way!"

In Jeremiah 9, God is telling us, *Make this – knowing me – the center of your life! Nothing else, nothing else, is more central, more urgent, more vital, more grand! Become one of my intimates! Here, right here, is your passion, your purpose, your privilege – that you know me!*

Sometimes I marvel at the attention we give the celebrities of our culture. We can be so enamored, so gushing. Yet, these movie stars, pro athletes, and business tycoons are mere humans, humans gifted by God. Here today, gone tomorrow. Grasshoppers. And all the while we are giving breathless attention to grasshoppers, we could have *God.* The God of the galaxies! The God of the cross! The God of love!

We aim too low. Way too low. In *The Weight of Glory,* C.S. Lewis makes this point.

> We are half-hearted creatures, fooling around with drink and sex and ambition when infinite joy is offered us, like an ignorant child who wants to go on making mud pies in a slum because he cannot imagine what is meant by the offer of a holiday at the sea. We are far too easily pleased. (p. 26)

About this time I obtained a copy of the book *Shadow of the Almighty.* It tells the story of Jim Elliot, who went to the jungles of Ecuador as a young man to reach a small tribe of Indians, the Aucas (now called, more properly, the Waorani). He and four other young men knew the risks they were taking because the tribe could be dangerous. However, compelled by Christ's love, they went to try to reach the tribe with the gospel. Tragically, all five were slaughtered by the Waorani, who would later come to Christ.

Jim Elliot's young widow, Elisabeth, compiled a book of his journals and letters. She called the book *Shadow of the Almighty* and it has marked my life. Jim Elliot knew God. When he was still a college student, at Wheaton College, he wrote the unforgettable words, "He is no fool who gives what he cannot keep to gain that which he cannot lose."

He also would write these lines about knowing God:

> Lord make my way prosperous, not that I achieve high station, but that my life may be an exhibit to the value of knowing God. *[Written when he was 20 years old.]*

> I walked out to the hill just now. It is exalting, delicious. To stand embraced by the shadows of a friendly tree with the wind tugging at your coattails and the heavens hailing your heart – to gaze and glory and to give oneself again to God, what more could a man ask? Oh the fullness, pleasure, sheer excitement of knowing God on earth. I care not if

I ever raise my voice again for Him, if only I may love Him, please Him. Mayhap in mercy He shall give me a host of children that I may lead through the vast star fields, to explore His delicacies, whose finger-ends set them to burning. But if not, if only I may see Him, touch His garments, and smile into my Lover's eyes – ah, then, not stars, nor children shall matter – only Himself.

Here is a man, young though he was, who knew and loved Jesus Christ. Do his words strike a chord in your heart? Do these words pierce your heart so deeply that you feel you might burst if you don't know God intimately? I hope so. I do hope so.

If you respond to God's call in Jeremiah 9, then what is your next step? What do you do?

A lot could be said and we should not be simplistic. This will not happen apart from a life of obedience, a life of holiness, a life of turning from sin in brokenness and repentance because you love God. But it also will not happen unless you take time each day to be with God, to draw close, to love him and receive his love, to sing and listen and confess and cry out and pour over the Bible. You simply will not become one of his intimates unless this unhurried time with God becomes a treasured part of your daily life. A.W. Tozer expressed this principle:

> May not the inadequacy of much of our spiritual experience be traced back to our habit of skipping through the corridors of the kingdom like children through the market place, chattering about everything but pausing to learn the true value of nothing.
>
> In my creature impatience I am often caused to wish that there were some way to bring modern Christians into a deeper spiritual life painlessly by short easy lessons. But such wishes are vain – no short cut exists. God has not bowed to our nervous haste, nor embraced the methods of our machine age. It is well that we accept the hard truth now. The man who would know God must give time to Him. (*The Divine Conquest*)

To know God is to love him, and to love God is to know him. Knowing God and loving God are all about intimacy with God and they go together. They are inseparable.

That brings us to the second foundational passage in Matthew 22. Whereas our first foundational passage, Jeremiah 9, uses the language of knowing God, our second foundational passage in Matthew 22 uses the language of loving God.

In Matthew 22, Jesus was asked about the greatest commandment. He answered immediately, quoting the great Shema passage in Deuteronomy 6. Jesus unequivocally answers that the greatest commandment is to love God! Here is the passage:

> But when the Pharisees heard that he had silenced
> the Sadducees, they gathered together. And one of
> them, a lawyer, asked him a question to test him.
> "Teacher, which is the great commandment in the
> Law?" And he said to him, "You shall love the Lord
> your God with all your heart and with all your soul
> and with all your mind. This is the great and first
> commandment. (22:34-38)

Above all else, God wants us to love him. Above all else, God wants us to love him back, and to love him back with all our heart and soul and strength and mind. God longs for us to love him passionately, fervently, wholeheartedly.

Mother Teresa, during a spiritually dry period of her life, once wrote this prayer in her journal, "I want to love you Jesus like you have never been loved before." *There it is!* This is the heart that God longs to see in each one of us. This is why we meet with God. It is because we want to love him like he's never been loved before. We want to know him, love him, be close to him.

The point of meeting with God is *not* to have a quiet time. That's never the point. The point is *God, God himself.* Loving God, knowing God, intimacy with God. The measure of the spiritual life is not a daily time with God. The measure of the spiritual life, as Jesus teaches us in Matthew 22, is loving God.

Time in the secret place, unhurried time alone with God, is the train that takes you to Jesus. This is the train that takes you to loving Jesus more. Meet with God because you thirst to know him. Meet with God because you long to love him more.

I cannot express how deeply I feel. This is what life is all about – knowing and loving God. This is why you and I are on the planet. This is *the* privilege of human life.

In 1978, as a young marathoner running with Nike's Athletics West Track Club, I ran the Boston Marathon. By God's grace, I finished second in 2:10:15, two seconds behind the winner, Bill Rodgers. That was, of course, extremely satisfying and exciting to me, but the thrill of finishing second in the Boston Marathon faded all too quickly. That thrill cannot be compared with the ever-growing thrill and privilege of knowing God. Any accomplishments I had in my running days mean nothing, less than nothing, compared to the privilege of knowing God. The same thing is true in every other area of life – wealth, looks, fame, power, education, house, everything. Nothing can fill the human heart except God himself.

Down through history, there have always been believers who loved God passionately, who knew God intimately. People like Augustine. Like A.W. Tozer. Like Jim Elliot. And countless others.

What about you? Will you become one of these intimates?

Will you seek the face of God? With all your heart and mind and soul? Are you one of those rare people who will refuse to be satisfied with anything less than God himself?

Go for it! Don't hold back! Pursue the Lord! Meet with him! Alone. Each day. To seek his face, to feel his touch, to glimpse his smile.

Why is this daily time with God so urgent, so important? Because we want to know God and to love him. This alone would be reason enough. More than enough. But there's more.

Chapter Three

I NEED THIS TIME

———————

The second reason that I make this time in the secret place a priority each day is because I *need* it. It's not just that I *want* to meet with God. I *need* to meet with God. I need this time for my sanity, for my soul restoration, for my emotional and mental and spiritual health. I need it for my survival.

In Psalm 23:3 David says of the Shepherd: "He restores my soul." I feel that God does that for me each day when I meet with him. It doesn't happen automatically. It doesn't happen if my mind is a million miles away. It doesn't happen if I hurry through the time to check a box. But if I immerse myself in his love, if I connect with him, if I open my heart to him and receive his love, if I love him back and draw close to him, if I worship and listen and call out to him, if I bring my burdens to him, he restores my soul.

I imagine that soul restoration is partly why Jesus made his time with the Father a priority. Consider Mark 1:35, *"And rising very early in the morning, while it was still dark, he departed and went out to a desolate place, and there he prayed."* The previous day was so busy with people crowding around him and clamoring for his attention, so he rose early the next morning and went out to a desolate place to pray, to restore his soul.

So often we think we can get restored by the weekend, or by television, or by a hobby or a sport, or by a vacation. Those things can help, but they are limited. They don't touch the soul. Only God can. For soul restoration we must connect with God. Augustine said it beautifully and poignantly: "You have made us for yourself O God, and our hearts are restless, until they find their rest in Thee."

Just about every day I drive to Burroughs Park, a nearby park with miles of forested trails. I run partly because I want to keep physically fit. I also run because I enjoy it; I like the sensation of physical movement and working hard. Moreover, I run because it is a stress reliever, especially after working a full day. But as much as I enjoy running and benefit from running, running itself doesn't touch the soul. It doesn't bring soul restoration. Only God can give us rest for our souls.

In Matthew 11:28, Jesus makes a remarkable statement: "Come to me, all who labor and are heavy laden, and I will give you rest." (Can you imagine any of the great philosophers, thinkers such as Aristotle or Descartes or Kant, saying this: "Come to me and I will give you rest"? Not hardly!) This unparalleled invitation applies to the non-Christian burdened by a load of sin. It also speaks to anyone, non-Christian or Christian, who is feeling overwhelmed by a crisis.

But the promise also applies to this unhurried time alone with God. Every day I have burdens and problems and challenges. Every day I struggle – with fear or anger or guilt or worry or conflict. There might be a big decision to make. Then there are all the problems and challenges of people around me, people I care about. To some extent, every day I am weary and burdened.

But Jesus bids me, "Come! Come to me! And I will give you rest. Give me your burden and I will give you my rest."

What a splendid, life-giving, soul-restoring offer!

I do not understand how Christians can function without this daily connecting with God. I would dry up and wither away. Or I would burn out. I *need* this. I want it, but I also need it.

I wonder if I need this time more than most believers because I struggled for decades with a mental condition, obsessive compulsive disorder. At times it has been painful, more painful than I can express. So perhaps I am a bit atypical in how much I need this time alone with God. When I say I need it for my sanity, this is not hyperbole. If my mental challenges have made me more dependent upon Christ, more desperate for Christ, then as painful as the struggle has been, I say to God: "Bless you, O Lord, for this struggle. Bless you, O Lord, for in my weaknesses I have been driven to you. And there you have met me and restored my weary soul."

David Bryant, author of *Christ Is All*, tells of visiting Mother Teresa in Calcutta. He was overwhelmed by the pain, poverty, and pathos that surrounded Mother Teresa and the other sisters in the order. So he asked her, "How do you do it? How do you keep going with these crushing needs all around you?" She replied, "Jesus is the deep well and I need to drop my bucket into the well every day."

Is that not a beautiful image of time with God? Jesus is the deep well. It's like a weary traveler in the desert drinking cool, refreshing, life-giving water from a well that is *continually* available.

In his book, *Reaching for the Invisible God*, Philip Yancey recalls a similar experience with Mother Teresa.

> I have visited Calcutta, India, a place of poverty, death, and irremediable human problems. There, the nuns trained by Mother Teresa serve the poorest, most miserable people on the planet: half-dead bodies picked up from the streets of Calcutta. The world stands in awe at the sisters' dedication and the results of their ministry, but something about these nuns

impresses me even more: their serenity. If I tackled such a daunting project, I would be scurrying about, faxing press releases to donors, begging for more resources, gulping tranquilizers, grasping at ways to cope with my mounting desperation. Not these nuns.

Their serenity traces back to what takes place before their day's work begins. At four o'clock in the morning, long before the sun, the sisters rise, awakened by a bell and the call, "Let us bless the Lord." "Thanks be to God," they reply. Dressed in spotless white saris, they file into the chapel, where they sit on the floor, Indian-style, and pray and sing together. On the wall of the plain chapel hangs a crucifix with the words, "I thirst." Before meeting their first "client," they immerse themselves in worship and in the love of God.

This is the essence of daily time with God: You immerse yourself in worship and in the love of God.

The second reason I meet with God daily is because I need it! How I need it. Because Jesus is the deep well and he's got the life-giving water. If there was no other reason to make time alone with God a priority, this would be enough. More than enough.

CHAPTER FOUR

I WANT THIS TIME

First of all, I want to love God more. Secondly, I need this time alone with God each day. Now thirdly, I *want* this time with God. It is not duty, but desire. I long to meet with him. I enjoy meeting with him. I yearn for him.

I don't claim my thirst for God is anything special. It should be so much greater. But a thirst for God is there and it compels me to seek God. This thirst, any thirst we have for God, is God's gift to us. Every good thing is a gift from God. *"What do you have that you have not received?" (1 Corinthians 4:7).* So this desire for God begins with God and it ends with God. It is God-given and it is God-driven.

We see this desire for God expressed in the Psalms.

> As a deer pants for flowing streams,
>   so pants my soul for you, O God.

My soul thirsts for God,
    for the living God.
When shall I come and appear before God?
(Psalm 42:1-2)

This is intense language! Emotional language! Personal language! *"Lord, just as a deer in the wilderness pants for water, thirsts for it, intensely craves it, Lord that's the way I feel about you. Lord, I need you! Lord, I thirst for you. Lord, I'm desperate for you! When can I come and meet with you, God? I've just got to have you!"*

The writer of Psalm 42 understood desire for God! He *wanted* God. He wanted to be *with* God. He did not merely want God's gifts. He wanted *God himself.*

Also, we see David's desire for God in Psalm 27.

One thing have I asked of the LORD,
    that will I seek after:
that I may dwell in the house of the LORD
    all the days of my life,
to gaze upon the beauty of the LORD
    and to inquire in his temple.
(Psalm 27:4)

This is desire for God, longing for God. *"O Lord, just let me be with you! Let me be near you! Let me see you and gaze upon your beauty! May I see your glory! Above all else, this is the one thing I desire! Lord!"*

This is the strong, personal, emphatic language of a person thirsting for God. For God himself, not for his gifts. This is thirst for God's face, not just for God's hand – that is, David thirsts for God himself and not just for God's gifts.

This is even more explicit a few verses later in Psalm 27.

> Hear, O LORD, when I cry aloud;
>> be gracious to me and answer me!
> You have said, "Seek my face."
> My heart says to you,
>> "Your face, LORD, do I seek."
> (Psalm 27:7-8)

God wants us to seek his face, to meet with him and draw close. David's heart resonates with God's desire. *"Yes, Lord! That's my heart! My heart says back to you, 'Your face, Lord, do I seek!'"*

One more example: Psalm 63 is a powerful example of this desire for God. It is probably my favorite Psalm.

> O God, you are my God; earnestly I seek you;
>> my soul thirsts for you;
> my flesh faints for you,
>> as in a dry and weary land where there is no water.
> (Psalm 63:1)

Do you feel David's heart, his passion, his intense thirst for God?

> O God, *you* are my God;
> *earnestly* I seek you;
> my soul *thirsts* for you;
> my flesh *faints* for you,
> as in a dry and weary land
>   where there is no water.
> *(emphasis added)*

Does David's passion stir something in you? Does it awaken longing in your heart for God? Do you feel what David is feeling?

David's passion for God is so strong that it affects not just his soul but his body.

> My soul thirsts for you;
> my *flesh* faints for you.
> *(emphasis added)*

I have been to the wilderness of Judah on several occasions and I can testify that it is a bleak and dry place. You could really get thirsty there! Yet David says: *Lord, that's the way I thirst for you – the way a thirsty man in the desert thirsts for water! Lord, I desperately want you! Desperately!*

David confesses that he seeks God *earnestly*. Not mechanically or casually or half-heartedly. But fervently, passionately, wholeheartedly. This is not religious duty! This is a love affair. This is not checking a performance box. This is not getting with God every few days when I have time and it's convenient. David is saying, "I need my God like I need oxygen!" *Earnestly!*

That's desire! Intense desire! And what makes this passage especially powerful is the dire circumstances when he wrote it. David is out in the wilderness, chased by enemies. His life is at stake. The kingdom is at stake. And yet here's David, more focused on God's face than on God's hand, more intent on seeking God for himself than what God can do for him. There's nothing wrong with asking things of God. David does that plenty, and we must do that if we are not self-reliant. But the priority is always God himself and not his gifts. That is what we see from David in Psalm 63.

The first eight verses of Psalm 63 continue to express intense longing and love for God. For example, verse 3:

> Because your steadfast love is better than life,
> my lips will praise you.

David felt *so* loved by God. This is the wellspring and the source of David's thirst for God. "Lord, your love is better than life itself. If I have to choose between you and life, I choose you Lord. I choose you!"

David is not just being dramatic. He is facing the real possibility of death. David's heart for God was a response to

God's deep and tender love for him. David felt so loved by God. Perhaps the strongest expression of how deeply David felt loved by God comes in Psalm 23. This is especially true of the final line in verse 6: *"Surely goodness and love will follow me all the days of my life, and I will dwell in the house of the Lord forever." (NASB)*

Let's look at one more verse in Psalm 63.

> My soul will be satisfied as with fat and rich food,
> and my mouth will praise you with joyful lips.
> (Psalm 63:5)

"Lord, you satisfy my soul the way food satisfies my appetite! And this isn't broccoli! This is Ben and Jerry's! This is blackberry cobbler with Blue Bell homemade vanilla ice cream! Lord, you are so good! You satisfy my soul!"

In fact, David felt this responsive love for God so deeply that he just had to praise God. "My lips will praise you." He could not *not* worship.

David's deepest desire was for God himself. What about you? What is your deepest desire? What do you long for? Does it involve your marriage or your kids or your career or your house or sports or your hobby or vacations or getting thinner? If your deepest desire is anything other than God, it won't be big enough. It won't satisfy your soul. Ecclesiastes 3:11 tells us that God has put eternity into man's heart. This means that God has made us for eternity and only eternal things can satisfy the human soul.

Bruce Marshall, in his book *The World, the Flesh, and Father Smith*, once remarked sagely, "Every time a man knocks on the door of a brothel he is looking for God." Marshall is insightful. What we really long for is not sex or drugs or alcohol or things or work. *Or anything else in this world.* Our deepest longings are for God himself.

When I consider Psalm 42 and Psalm 27 and Psalm 63, I think of a quote by Augustine, the renowned fourth-century theologian:

> Give me a man in love; he knows what I mean. Give me one who yearns; give me one who is hungry; give me one far away in this desert, who is thirsty and sighs for the spring of the Eternal Country. Give me that sort of man; he knows what I mean. But if I speak to a cold man, he just doesn't know what I am talking about.

A third reason that I meet with God daily is because I want to. I long for God and I want to meet with him. Of course my longing is too small, but still, I long for him and thirst for him. I *want* to meet with him. For God himself and not for anything he gives me. I want him, his love, his mercy, his presence.

If there were no other reasons than this, to make time in the secret place a priority, this would be enough. More than enough. But there is more.

CHAPTER FIVE

GOD WANTS THIS TIME

———————

The fourth reason I meet alone with God is because God wants it. He desires it. This is the miracle. Think of it: The sovereign, infinite, holy God, the God who created hundreds of billions of galaxies by his mere breath, the God who is so vast and immense as to be incomprehensible to our puny minds, the God of all glory, the King and Judge of the universe, this God wants to meet alone with *me*. With *you*.

Amazing.

Nearly unbelievable. But yet the Bible tells us, from Genesis to Revelation, that our God cares about us. He cares about us so much that he's numbered the hairs on our head. More importantly, he cares about us so much that he sent his only Son to die for us on a cross thereby redeeming us. *But God shows his love for us in that while we were still sinners, Christ died for us (Romans 5:8).*

There is no greater theme in all the Bible than God's love for us, God's redeeming love for us in Christ Jesus. We see this love throughout the Old Testament and throughout the New Testament. We see this love pursuing Adam and Eve when they had rebelled against God and were hiding from him. We see this love in his repeated grace to Abraham, Isaac, Jacob and Joseph. We see this love redeeming the people of Israel from slavery in Egypt and rescuing them through the Red Sea. We see it throughout the Psalms. There we see God as the Shepherd who cares intensely for us and gives us good things and protects us. The Shepherd who never leaves us. The Shepherd who will pursue us with love and mercy for the rest of our lives. We see God's love throughout the prophets, especially when Hosea continues to pursue his wayward wife Gomer, just as God pursues his wayward wife, the people of Israel.

We see God's love for us throughout the Old Testament. And then when we turn to the New Testament we continue to see it. We see it in the tender compassion that Jesus has for the leper when he reaches out to touch the leper before he heals him (Matthew 8). We see it in his deep compassion for the widow of Nain, who had just lost her only son (Luke 7). We see it in his heartfelt compassion for the helpless multitudes who are like sheep without a shepherd (Matthew 9).

We certainly see God's love in the story of the Prodigal Son, where Jesus pictures God as a father running after his rebel son, and then smothering his long lost son with kisses and hugs. He forgives this prodigal son completely and restores him fully to his sonship. In fact, is there a more beautiful portrait of God's love for us in all the Bible than this father pursuing his prodigal son in Luke 15? Consider especially verse 20: "And he arose and came to his father. But while he was still a long way off, his father saw him and felt compassion, and ran and embraced him and kissed him."

But, above all, we see God's love for us in the cross of Jesus, where God, God the Son, hangs on a cross, dying for sin – for *our* sin, for *your* sin, for *my* sin. Because of his great love for us.

J.I. Packer, theologian and writer, reminds us that the primary name for God in the New Testament is Father. Yes, he's Father. Papa. Daddy. He's the perfect Father, who is crazy about his kids.

Does Papa desire to spend time with you? Intimate time? Personal time? Loving time? Challenging time? O yes! More than you can imagine.

Just as I want to spend time with my kids and my grandkids, and they want to spend time with me, so Papa wants to spend time with us. And he loves it when we also want to spend time with him.

After all, the Bible does not give us religion. This is love, not religion. A Father's love. A child's love. Loving and being loved.

Papa doesn't want you to meet with him out of duty, but out of love. He loves you and he longs for you to love him back.

This is the fourth reason that this time with God is a priority: because God desires it. He wants it. If there were no other reason, this would be reason enough. More than reason enough. But there is more.

Chapter Six

THE EXAMPLE OF JESUS

———————

When it comes to time alone with God, we need to look at the life of Jesus. Did Jesus meet alone with the Father to draw close? Was Jesus a man of prayer? Did he treasure and read the Scriptures? Was this time a priority for Jesus?

Earlier I noted that Mark 1 describes an extremely full day for Jesus. He teaches in the synagogue (1:21). There he also has a confrontation with a demon and casts the demon out of a man (1:26). He then goes to the home of Peter's mother-in-law, where he heals her of a fever (1:31). Perhaps there are other demands placed upon him during the afternoon hours. But in the evening, people start showing up at the door of Peter's mother-in-law, clamoring for Jesus' help. Pretty soon, the whole city has gathered, bringing the sick and those oppressed by demons. Jesus heals them all and casts out every demon (1:32-34). No one was turned away. Perhaps Jesus spent hours tirelessly ministering to the crowds.

That kind of day exacts a heavy toll – pouring your heart out in teaching, confronting demons, healing scores of people, having people all around you wanting your time, your help, your attention. Jesus must have been exhausted!

It would be understandable if he took the next day off or at least slept late to recover from the grueling Sabbath day. But what does the next verse tell us? "And rising very early in the morning, while it was still dark, he departed and went out to a desolate place, and there he prayed" (Mark 1:35). He rises early. *Very* early. Long before sunrise. He leaves the house and goes to find a secluded place, a secret place, so he can be alone with his Father.

Apparently, this time alone with the Father was so valuable to Jesus, so essential to his spiritual and emotional health, that it was an urgent priority, even after an extremely busy day.

God is giving us an indication of what this time in the secret meant to Jesus – and what it should mean to us.

Then there's Luke's Gospel, which emphasizes the importance of prayer – especially the priority of prayer in the life of Jesus. Here are just some of the examples.

"But he would withdraw to desolate places and pray" (Luke 5:16). Jesus would regularly withdraw from people to find time in the secret place with the Father. This was Jesus' custom, his

practice, just like with the example of Mark 1:35. Luke 5:16 was not atypical, but rather typical of the way Jesus lived his life.

"In these days he went out to the mountain to pray, and all night he continued in prayer to God" (Luke 6:12). This was a special occasion. Jesus was about to select his inner group of twelve disciples. And so he prayed *all night.*

"Now it happened that as he was praying alone, the disciples were with him" (Luke 9:18a). Again, Luke indicates the priority of prayer for Jesus. This is just the way Jesus lived his life. It was normal.

"Now about eight days after these sayings he took with him Peter and John and James and went up on the mountain to pray" (Luke 9:28). He's getting away from the crowds, away from most of the disciples. To talk with the Father. Again, this was the way he lived his life.

"Now Jesus was praying in a certain place, and when he finished, one of his disciples said to him, 'Lord, teach us to pray, as John taught his disciples'" (Luke 11:1). Again we find Jesus praying. This time, one of the disciples asks him, "Lord, teach us to pray." It is significant that we know of no occasion where the disciples ask Jesus to teach them to preach or lead or heal or cast out demons. But Jesus' prayer was so compelling, so powerful, so extraordinary, that they could not hold back: "Lord, teach us to pray!"

"And he told them a parable to the effect that they ought always to pray and not lose heart" (Luke 18:1). Jesus teaches us to always pray and not grow discouraged if we don't get the answer we want when we want it. Keep on praying! Never give up praying!

"It is written, 'My house shall be a house of prayer,' but you have made it a den of robbers" (Luke 19:46). Jesus teaches us that prayer is so important that the essence of the temple is to be a house of prayer. Not a house of teaching. Not a house of scholarship. Not a house of sacrifice. Not a house of worship. But a house of prayer. That's the central purpose!

Prayer was a priority to Jesus, because the Father was a priority to Jesus. His main priority. Jesus lived a life of prayer. He was always praying. He was forever going off by himself, to get time in the secret place with the Father. At times, he would even spend hours alone with God.

Jesus is showing us how to live life. If it was a priority for him, should it not be a priority for us? If it was an urgent matter for him, should it not be an urgent matter for us? If he needed this regular time of prayer, do we not need it? If Jesus longed for this time, should we not long for it? If it was essential for him, should it not be essential for us?

What about the Bible? Was the Bible (our Old Testament) important to him? We would love more details about Jesus reading the Scriptures but this is what we see in the Gospels:

Jesus knew the Scriptures. He quoted the Scriptures. He studied the Scriptures. He loved the Scriptures. Every time Jesus refers to the Bible he does so with complete confidence in the authority and the veracity of Scripture. For Jesus, if the Bible said it, then God said it.

But Jesus did not merely know the Bible and read the Bible and trust the Bible. He *obeyed* the Bible. For example, when Jesus was tempted in the wilderness, with each temptation he quotes Scripture, from memory. And he obeys that passage. He doesn't simply *know* Scripture. He *submits* to Scripture.

Perhaps the best word to describe Jesus' attitude to the Bible is the word *treasure*. Jesus treasured the Bible. He treasured the Bible as the Word of God not the words of man. We don't know that Jesus walked around Israel carrying a scroll or scrolls. The Bible was not so portable as it is today. But Jesus carried the Bible in his heart. And he treasured it.

Was Scripture important to Jesus? Oh yes! Unmistakably. Just like prayer was vital to Jesus. Time alone with the Father, talking, listening, drawing close, just being with his Father, was absolutely vital to Jesus.

One final passage to consider in the life of Jesus is the brief anecdote of Martha and Mary in Luke 10.

> Now as they went on their way, Jesus entered a village. And a woman named Martha welcomed him

> into her house. And she had a sister called Mary, who
> sat at the Lord's feet and listened to his teaching. But
> Martha was distracted with much serving. And she
> went up to him and said, "Lord, do you not care that
> my sister has left me to serve alone? Tell her then
> to help me." But the Lord answered her, "Martha,
> Martha, you are anxious and troubled about many
> things, but one thing is necessary. Mary has chosen
> the good portion, which will not be taken away from
> her." (Luke 10:38-42)

Can you imagine this scene? Martha is in the kitchen, a blur
of activity and effort to serve Jesus and his disciples. And
where's her sister Mary? In the other room! With the men!
Sitting at the feet of Jesus!

Finally Martha's frustration level boils over and she confronts
Jesus about her sister Mary *not* helping. In one sentence she
manages to rebuke both Jesus and Mary! "Lord do you not
care that my sister has left me to serve alone? Tell her then
to help me."

But Jesus, never a pleaser, said no. "Martha, one thing is
necessary. Mary has chosen the best thing, just being with me,
listening to me, seeking me. And no, I won't take that away."

For many Christians, this passage bothers them. It's not fair!
We buy into the American mindset that we must be *doing*
something. "Don't just sit there! Do something!" But we can

neglect the inner life, the life of the heart, if we are always doing something.

There is a time to serve Jesus, to *do* things for Jesus. But there's also a time to simply *be* with Jesus, to seek his face.

In this remarkable passage, Jesus teaches us the priority of just being with him, because we love him and want to love him more. Jesus is looking, not primarily for workers, but for worshipers. Like Martha, we often assume that *doing* for Jesus is more important than *being* with Jesus. There are many people who are workers, *doing* for Jesus. There are far fewer who are worshipers, *being* with Jesus. In Luke 10:38-42, Jesus gives us his perspective about time alone with God, sitting at his feet, seeking his face. This, Jesus says, is the good part, the necessary part. And it won't be taken away.

In the Gospels we see how much Jesus valued prayer, how much he valued God's Word, how much he values time alone with the Father.

Chapter Seven

A STRANGE RELUCTANCE

Despite the compelling reasons to meet with God, and despite the strong example of Jesus, there still seems to be a strange reluctance with Christians to meet with God daily in the secret place.

Just about every believer will affirm the four reasons I have outlined to be with the Lord – I long to be with him, God longs for me to be with him, I want to love God more and know him better, I need this time for my emotional and spiritual health.

But yet, the vast majority of Christ-followers spend little time or even no time alone with the Lord. Why is this?

John R.W. Stott was a long-time pastor in London who was deep with the Lord. I am confident that his time with God was a daily priority. Yet he acknowledges the internal resistance at times:

> The thing I know will give me the deepest joy –
> namely, to be alone and unhurried in the presence
> of God, aware of His presence, my heart open to
> worship Him – is often the thing I least want to do.

J. Oswald Sanders, who became the President of Overseas
Missionary Fellowship (the remarkable ministry founded by
Hudson Taylor as the China Inland Mission) and wrote the
classic book, *Spiritual Leadership*, addressed this issue:

> Christ is claiming the ability to satisfy the deepest
> need of the human heart, yet we are strangely
> reluctant to come directly to Him. We will attend
> ceremonies and observe sacraments. We will follow
> men and congregate in meetings. We will frequent
> camps and conventions.
>
> We will listen to priests and preachers – anything, it
> would seem, except come personally and alone into
> the presence of Christ. But He is absolutely intolerant.
> He will quench our spiritual thirst personally and not
> by proxy.

Then there's the testimony of the famed British pastor, Samuel
Chadwick, about the silent spaces of the soul:

> It is in them we learn to pray. There, alone, shut in
> with God, our Lord bids us pray to our Father who

is in secret, and seeth in secret. There is no test like solitude ... The heart shrinks from being alone with God ... It would revolutionize the lives of most [people] if they were shut in with God in some secret place for half an hour a day. (Quoted by Gordon MacDonald in *The Life God Blesses*)

I have to face up to my own reluctance: "Why do I so often meet with God more out of duty than delight, more out of discipline than desire? What is the source of my reluctance?"

What is behind this "strange reluctance," as Sanders calls it? What is the root of the heart shrinking from being alone with God, as Chadwick puts it? I don't think it's clear, but there are a number of possibilities.

Do we forget who we are and who God is? Do we forget that we are God's much-loved, blood-bought children and that he is our loving Father? Do we forget that our sins are cleansed by the blood of Christ and that we can run into his presence at any time and jump into his lap?

Do we listen to the voice of the enemy, the accuser of the brothers (as he is called in Revelation 12:11)? Do we allow Satan to heap guilt upon us, tell us we are unworthy to come into God's presence, whisper that God is not good and cannot be trusted? Do we allow the devil to deceive us, discourage us and thereby devour us? If so, shut your ears to those lies! Recognize that Satan is fine with your religious duty, but detests you meeting with God to love him.

Maybe the problem is our anger. Our anger at God. Maybe we are angry at God because of the way our life has turned out or because he hasn't answered a certain prayer the way we wanted or because of pain we've experienced. Perhaps we are angry at God but we are not honest with ourselves or with God about that anger – even though God loves us to be honest with him.

Perhaps we have unrealistic expectations. Perhaps we are expecting a dramatic encounter or bolt of lightning every day. Maybe we lack endurance and fail to realize that time with God in the secret will pay its richest dividends over the long haul, that the spiritual life is a marathon not a 100-meter sprint.

Perhaps the issue is laziness. This time can be an immense delight, but it can also be work. It takes energy to think and pray and study and intercede. Epaphras labored in prayer for the Colossian believers. He agonized. He worked hard. "Epaphras, who is one of you, a servant of Christ Jesus, greets you, always struggling on your behalf in his prayers, that you may stand mature and fully assured in all the will of God. For I bear him witness that he has worked hard for you and for those in Laodicea and in Hierapolis" (Colossians 4:12-13).

Perhaps we are afraid of silence and solitude and stillness. Maybe we need to immerse ourselves in noise and activity and a continual stream of people because we are running from the pain of loneliness or guilt, rather than bringing our burdens to Jesus and receiving his rest. (Matthew 11:28: "Come to me, all who labor and are heavy laden, and I will give you rest.")

Maybe the problem is simpler: Do I go to bed too late? Do I simply not discipline myself to go to bed at a decent time so I can get up early and meet with God? (This time does not have to be in the morning, but for most people it will be.)

Is the problem that I don't fully appreciate the incredible privilege of meeting with the Almighty? Do I fail to realize that he longs to meet with me? That I desperately need this time?

For many people, perhaps the main problem is that we allow ourselves to be distracted by other things, even good things. The classic example of this is found in Luke 10 which we saw earlier. "Martha was distracted with much serving" (Luke 10:40a). Martha meant well. She was serving Jesus. But Mary had chosen the best thing: seeking the *face* of Jesus, sitting at his feet. We can easily make the mistake of Martha, allowing ourselves to be preoccupied with anything other than sitting at the feet of Jesus.

For some people the problem may be that their relationship with God is more head than heart. I can remember when I was a young pastor in Oregon. I was about 30 years old and I realized that I did not feel deeply loved by God. I preached

about God's love and I read about God's love, but at a deep
level, I did not *feel* loved by God.

When I came to this painful realization, I set out on a journey.
A desperate journey. A journey to experience God's love
personally. I began praying fervently that God would show
me his love. When I read the Bible, I began looking for verses
about the tenderness and kindness and grace and love and
forgiveness of God. I became alert for those things.

In my journey, God really used music to draw me close. At
this time there was a transition happening in the church from
traditional hymns to contemporary Christian music. The
biggest difference for me was a transition from singing *about*
God to singing *to* God. This simple but powerful transition
impacted my heart significantly.

With all of this and more, and over a long period of time, God
transformed me. Perhaps it was not until 15 years later that I
realized that I now felt deeply loved by God. And it has made
all the difference.

If our relationship with God is simply academic or cerebral
and does not deeply touch the heart, so that we *experience*
God's love for us, then we are missing out, my friends!

If this is the case, we might lack a deep desire to meet with
God. To the extent that we feel a deep, passionate yearning
for God, to that extent we will want to meet with him and

draw close.

Do any of these apply to you? I don't know and you may not know either. But God knows. Talk with him. Ask him. Then be still and listen for his voice.

Be aware of this strange reluctance to be alone in God's presence, a human reluctance exacerbated by the enemy. Don't surrender to this tendency! Ask God to give you grace to run gladly into his presence, day after day after day. He waits with open arms.

PART II

GETTING PRACTICAL

CHAPTER EIGHT

PRACTICAL GUIDELINES

―――――――

It's time to get more practical. How do you go about this time with God? I have four practical suggestions on what to do.

Firstly, make a decision. Make a decision that this will be part of your daily life. If any of my four reasons are true for you – you love God and want this time alone with him, you know God wants this time with you, you long to know him more and love him more, you need this time for soul restoration and survival – if *any* of these reasons are true for you, then decide to go for it. Decide: "Lord, I am going to get alone with you every day, to meet you and draw close to you. O Lord, guide me, draw me, meet with me. Protect me from legalism or religious duty. But, O Lord, give me grace to seek your face, to receive your love, to love you back. In the name of Jesus, I pray. Amen." Start here. Pre-decide for all your days so you don't have to decide each day.

Earlier I mentioned that I had been a serious distance runner as a young man. I ran track in college at Rice and then I ran marathons for a Nike track club, Athletics West. During these years I ran a lot of miles, often about 100 miles per week or more. But one thing I did *not* do. I did not wake up and decide, "Should I run today or not?" No, that was a given. That was already decided. If you are seeking to run with the best marathoners in the world, then you'd better show up every day and run. This mindset helped. The basic decision had already been made. Similarly, we must make the decision: "I will meet with God every day. For all kinds of good reasons, I will do this. Not because of duty or obligation, but because of love and longing, I will meet with God."

Research shows that we are significantly more likely to keep a commitment if we pre-decide to keep it than if we just decide to do something in the moment. For example, you set the alarm for 6 a.m. before you go to sleep, and you pre-decide: "I am going to get up as soon as I hear the alarm. I am not going to hit snooze or turn the alarm off." If you pre-decide the night before you are much more likely to get up. The same is true in meeting with God. Pre-decide that you're going to do this every day.

Secondly, decide what you will give up. Oswald Chambers has had enormous influence around the world through his book of daily devotionals, *My Utmost for His Highest.* He once stated:

It is impossible for a believer, no matter what his experience, to keep right with God if he will not take the trouble to spend time with God. Spend plenty of time with God; let other things go, but don't neglect Him.

Chambers was wise. It is impossible to keep a healthy, thriving, joy-filled relationship with God unless we spend plenty of time with God. But the critical point is his last one: "Let other things go, but don't neglect Him."

What things can you give up? What good thing can you give up? Maybe you give up the nightly news, or ESPN, or a half-hour of television. Maybe you limit your time on Facebook or Instagram or other social media. Perhaps you spend less time with work or less time with the newspaper. Ask the Lord: "Papa, what can I give up?"

You have time to do the things that you really need to do.

Thirdly, set a time and place. This is your default time and place. I'm a morning person, so for me this is the first thing when I wake up. I quickly get dressed and drive five minutes to work while it is still dark. There, alone in our office building, I can walk the halls and sip coffee and talk with God. I walk all over our building, and at times roam outside the building. Sometimes I sit, but not that much. My default time and place to meet with God is our office building. In the early morning hours I am there alone and I love it. It fits the way

God made me.

For you, it might be your favorite chair in the living room after breakfast. Or perhaps you drive to work a half-hour early and close your door. Or, you go into your study each night before bedtime.

What works for you? When are you most alert and alive? Where can you be least interrupted and silence your cell phone?

My fourth and final suggestion: *Decide on your basic approach or format.* What are you actually going to do during this time?

I hesitate here. Perhaps this is what you are most interested in and I can understand that. But this time is personal, not mechanistic or formulaic. You are meeting with a person. This is not: "Follow these four steps." Moreover, we each need to find our own approach, our own thumbprint, the way we best connect with God. After all, that's the point: Connect with God.

But still it may be helpful to hear a few examples to get ideas. I'll begin with my own practice.

I begin by immersing myself in God's love and worship. I will often pray: "Father, I love you. Jesus, I love you. Spirit, I love you." I might also pray: "Good morning, Father. Good morning, Jesus. Good morning, Spirit." I'll ask God to speak to me and meet with me. There will be a time of adoration, thanksgiving, worship. Just about always I will sing a song to the Lord. (This time of singing is very important to me. God loves my voice – though he's the only one!) Sometimes I'll play a favorite worship song. Often I remind myself of the truths of the Bible about God's love for me and how all my sins are nailed to the cross and covered by Christ's blood. I might go over some verses, such as these:

"In this is love, not that we have loved God but that he loved us and sent his Son to be the propitiation for our sins" (1 John 4:10).

"There is no fear in love, but perfect love casts out fear. For fear has to do with punishment, and whoever fears has not been perfected in love" (1 John 4:18).

"There is therefore now no condemnation for those who are in Christ Jesus" (Romans 8:1).

"For those whom he foreknew he also predestined to be conformed to the image of his Son, in order that he might be the firstborn among many brothers. And those whom he predestined he also called, and those whom he called he also justified, and those whom he justified he also glorified" (Romans 8:29-30).

"He has delivered us from the domain of darkness and transferred us to the kingdom of his beloved Son, in whom we have redemption, the forgiveness of sins" (Colossians 1:13-

14).

This is a time to glory in God's love and grace to me. I let God love me and I love him back!

Then I normally spend time in listening prayer. I seek to silence my tongue and my mind. (Silencing my mind is not easy for me.) I'll ask God to speak to me and then be quiet. Or I might ask God a specific question. For example, "Lord is there anything I need to know about this problem?" Or, "Lord what do you want to say to me today?" If I sense God putting something on my heart then I'll jot that down on my journal for listening prayer. Sometimes I don't get anything. At other times I get something simple and practical, such as: "Be more attentive with Gayle today."

After some time, I open the Bible. I don't rush this time. I read slowly, I am praying as I read. I look at this time, not so much as reading through the Bible, but also praying through the Bible. This is a time to meet God in the Bible.

Finally, there's a time of petition and intercession. I pray for my immediate family by name (13 of us currently: Gayle, three kids and their spouses which I consider to be six kids, five grandkids and me). I pray especially that we would love God, trust God, know God, obey God, hear God, fear God, enjoy God. But I also pray for our marriages, parenting, ministry, work, healing and more. I also pray for extended family, for close friends, for our church. I pray for lost people that God has put on my heart. (At our church, I ask people to pray daily for their Top Five friends who may not know Christ.) I pray for fellow elders, fellow pastors on our team and in the city. There are so many people to pray for!

That's my current practice. I say current practice because this time with God is ever-evolving. At least it has for the last 47 years. I tweak it here or I tweak it there. More time here or more time there. The order might change some. There is no formula. We are meeting with our God. The main thing is just to *be together*. Be together and draw close.

Here is another example, that of George Müller. Müller lived an incredible life. He pastored the same church in Bristol, England, for 60 years during the 1800s. He founded an orphanage and provided for thousands of orphans and never asked anyone for money. Yet his orphans never missed a meal. He founded the orphanage, not so much to take care of the orphans, but to provide an example to Christians that God is a prayer-hearing God. Most importantly, Müller *knew* God. Intimately. This was Müller's approach in his time with God, as seen in his autobiography. Note the emphasis on Scripture though he was known as a man of prayer.

> The primary business I must attend to every day is to fellowship with the Lord. The first concern is not how much I might serve the Lord, but how my inner man might be nourished. I may share the truth with the

unconverted; I may try to encourage believers; I may relieve the distressed; or I may, in other ways, seek to behave as a child of God; yet, not being happy in the Lord and not being nourished and strengthened in my inner man day by day, may result in this work being done in the wrong spirit.

The most important thing I had to do was to read the Word of God and to meditate on it. Thus my heart might be comforted, encouraged, warned, reproved, and instructed.

Formerly, when I rose, I began to pray as soon as possible. But I often spent a quarter of an hour to an hour on my knees struggling to pray while my mind wandered. Now I rarely have this problem. As my heart is nourished by the truth of the Word, I am brought into true fellowship with God. I speak to my Father and to my Friend (although I am unworthy) about the things that He has brought before me in His precious Word.

It often astonishes me that I did not see the importance of meditation upon Scripture earlier in my Christian life. As the outward man is not fit for work for any length of time unless he eats, so it is with the inner man. What is the food for the inner man? Not prayer, but the Word of God – not the

simple reading of the Word of God, so that it only
passes through our minds, just as water runs through
a pipe. No, we must consider what we read, ponder
over it, and apply it to our hearts. (p. 138)

That was Müller's practice.

It's vital that you find *your* spiritual thumbprint. What works
best for you? How has God wired you? Is there more singing?
More reading in the Bible? More listening? Do you start with
petition? Find your rhythm. Ask the Lord to guide you.

I appreciate Brennan Manning's point in *The Ragamuffin
Gospel*, where he stresses that we cannot do this badly. "A little
child cannot do a bad coloring; nor can a child of God do bad
prayer." He then quotes M. Basil Pennington:

A father is delighted when his little one, leaving off
her toys and friends, runs to him and climbs into
his arms. As he holds his little one close to him,
he cares little whether the child is looking around,
her attention flitting from one thing to another,
or just settling down to sleep. Essentially the child
is choosing to be with her father, confident of the
love, the care, the security that is hers in those arms.
Our prayer is much like that. We settle down in our
Father's arms, in His loving hands. Our mind, our
thoughts, our imagination may flit about here and
there; we might even fall asleep; but essentially we

are choosing for this time to remain intimately with our Father, giving ourselves to Him, receiving His love and care, letting Him enjoy us as He will. It is very simple prayer. It is prayer that opens us out to all the delights of the kingdom.

How encouraging!

My four suggestions:

Make a decision to do this.

Decide what you will give up.

Set a time and place.

Decide on your basic approach.

There are few men in history that God has used as significantly as John Wesley. During the 1700s, this British Christian leader had enormous impact on both sides of the Atlantic Ocean. God would use him to begin the Methodist Church, and in many ways, changed the fabric of everyday life in Britain.

The foundation of all that he accomplished was his own personal love relationship with Jesus. He knew that his unhurried time with God was essential.

This was his charge to his followers:

O begin! Fix some part of every day for private exercises ... Whether you like it or not, read and pray daily. It is for your life; there is no other way: else you will be a trifler all your days.

"O begin!" Do not wait another day! "O begin!"

"Fix some part of every day." Predecide when you will meet with God each day.

"Whether you like it or not." The issue is not what you like to do, but what you need to do and what God wants you to do.

"It is for your life." There is no real abundant life apart from cultivating this love relationship with God. "There is no other way."

"Else you will be a trifler all your days." A trifler! A dilettante! An amateur! If this is not your daily practice, then you are just messing around with God. You are not serious about knowing and loving your God. You will simply be a trifler with the things of God!

O begin! This is for your life!

CHAPTER NINE

HEART ATTITUDES

The attitudes and perspectives with which we come to God make all the difference. Here are six essential heart attitudes, some of which I have alluded to in previous chapters.

First of all, the purpose of this time with the Lord is not to learn theology but to meet God. We will learn theology. We will acquire biblical knowledge. But that's never the primary purpose.

The purpose is God himself – to meet God, to encounter God, to experience God, to know God, to love God. The focus is not so much on the Word of God but on the God of the Word.

Biblical knowledge can be intoxicating. It can make me feel more spiritual. It can make me feel pleasing to God. It can make me feel superior to other Christians. In other words, biblical knowledge can easily lead to spiritual pride. That's why Paul remarked that "knowledge puffs up" (1 Corinthians 8:1).

Life is not found in the Bible itself. That is, life is not found in biblical knowledge. Life is found in Jesus. The Bible has value only if it leads us to Jesus. There are many people who know the Bible who don't know Jesus.

So go beyond the page to the person, the person of Jesus. Open the Bible and look for Jesus. Open the Bible and hear the voice of Jesus. Open the Bible in order to meet Jesus. Enter the presence of God.

The renowned artist Vincent Van Gogh once wrote in a letter to his sister: "You read books to borrow therefrom the force to stimulate your activity … but I read books searching for the man who has written them." If that's true for books in general, it is certainly true for this Book.

In the classic book, *The Pursuit of God,* A.W. Tozer makes a point about preaching that applies to this time alone with God:

> Sound Bible exposition is an imperative must in the Church of the Living God. But exposition may be carried on in such a way as to leave the hearers devoid of any true spiritual nourishment whatever. For it is not mere words that nourish the soul, but God

Himself, and unless and until the hearers find God in personal experience they are not the better for having heard the truth. The Bible is not an end in itself, but a means to bring men to an intimate and satisfying knowledge of God, that they may enter into Him, that they may delight in His Presence, may taste and know the inner sweetness of the very God Himself in the core and center of their hearts.

(*The Pursuit of God*, p. 9)

This time with God is more about *being* than *doing*. This is not an activity to *do*, but a time to *be* with the Lord, to love him, to adore him, to enjoy him, to seek his face. David gives us the essential perspective in Psalm 27:8: "You have said, 'Seek my face.' My heart says to you, 'Your face, LORD, do I seek.'"

Secondly, come to God not for information, but for transformation. This is similar to the first principle, but it is nuanced. The first principle is this: Focus on knowing God, not the Bible. The second principle is: Focus on transformation, not information. We don't meet with God to gain information about the Bible, but to have our lives transformed, to become more like Jesus Christ.

The purpose is not greater knowledge but greater love. Certainly we want more knowledge about God, but mostly we want the Lord to transform us into the image of Jesus Christ. (See Romans 8:29) The ultimate focus is not our heads but our hearts.

Rodney Smith put it this way: "What makes the difference is not how many times you have been through the Bible but how many times and how thoroughly the Bible has been through you."

Sören Kierkegaard made a similar point when he said, "When you read God's Word, you must constantly be saying to yourself, 'It is talking to me and about me.'" The goal is not more information, but life transformation.

Thirdly, come to God not out of spiritual pride, but out of profound humility. Come with a broken and humble heart, tender before God. Come with the prayer: "Lord, teach me. Lord, change me. Lord, speak to me. Lord, I am desperate for you."

Come, not because you are so spiritual but because you want to become spiritual, because you have so far to go. Come with an open and humble heart.

The Pharisees studied the Scriptures, but they came to the Bible with spiritual pride and self-righteousness, not with humility and brokenness. Not surprisingly, they missed God!

God calls us to humility before the word: "*Humbly* accept the word planted in you" (James 1:21, NIV, *emphasis added*).

Humility means that we will not approach the Bible to

critique and judge, but to let the Bible judge us. In his book *Authentic Christianity,* John Stott challenges us:

> We need to repent of the haughty way in which we sometimes stand in judgement upon Scripture and must learn to sit humbly under its judgement instead. If we come to Scripture with our minds made up, expecting to hear from it only an echo of our own thoughts and never the thunderclap of God's, then indeed he will not speak to us and we shall only be confirmed in our own prejudices. We must allow the Word of God to confront us, to disturb our security, to undermine our complacency and to overthrow our patterns of thought and behavior.

Come to God out of deep and genuine humility.

Fourthly, come to the Lord not out of discipline and duty, but out of love. This time with God is all about love. It's all about a love relationship. We come to God because he loves us and we love him back. (God's love is always prior to our love.) We come to God because we want to love him more.

This is a time to immerse yourself in God's love. This is a time to go over verses on God's love for you, to rejoice in God's love for you, to sing of God's love for you, to delight in God's love for you. This is a time to remember that all your sins were nailed to the cross and that your sins have been removed from you as far as the east is from the west. (See Colossians 2:13-14 and Psalm 103:12.)

This is a time to let God love you and love him back. In a time of prayer once, I felt God gave me the picture of being wrapped snugly in a blanket as an image of his love for me. That is an endearing picture of God's love for me. I'm letting God love me. I'm soaking in God's love. I'm delighting in God's great love for me.

Be very clear with yourself: This is not religious performance or religious duty. You are not earning God's love. You are not earning God's approval. You are not earning brownie points with God. You are spending time with God *not to gain his love, but because he already loves you.* Perfectly. Intensely. Tenderly. Emotionally. In fact, he will never love you any more or any less than he loves you right now. This very moment. You are secure in the embrace of God's great love for you!

Go over and over passages in the Bible like Romans 8:37-39: "No, in all these things we are more than conquerors through him who loved us. For I am sure that neither death nor life, nor angels nor rulers, nor things present nor things to come, nor powers, nor height nor depth, nor anything else in all creation, will be able to separate us from the love of God in Christ Jesus our Lord."

This time with the Father is not about religion. It's not about performance. It's a love affair. Get lost in the wonder of God's love and mercy!

Fifthly, come to God with an unhurried spirit. Don't rush through this time to check your box and move on. Slow down. Savor. Enjoy the Lord.

Henry Blackaby, the author of the workbook *Experiencing God*, which had enormous impact in the 1990s, told this story. "I was in my study and I sensed God saying, 'You're hurrying me.' I was so busy with the work of the church. I sensed God saying to me, 'You are not going to hurry me anymore.' So I began getting up at 4:30 a.m. and I took as much time with God as God wanted. Then I began to do the task of ministry."

My point in this anecdote is not 4:30 a.m. or unlimited time, but hurrying God. Whatever time you have, do not hurry your way through it.

In the superb biography, *Hudson's Taylor's Spiritual Secret* (I am a biography lover and this is perhaps my favorite biography), there is a quote from the godly South African pastor, Andrew Murray.

> Take time. Give God time to reveal Himself to you. Give yourself time to be silent and quiet before Him, waiting to receive, through the Spirit, the assurance of His presence with you, His power working in you. Take time to read His Word as in His presence, that from it you may know what He asks of you and what He promises you. Let the Word create around you, create within you a holy atmosphere, a holy

heavenly light, in which your soul will be refreshed and strengthened for the week of daily life.

Take time. Give the Lord time.

When I talk about this time with God to the people of WoodsEdge Community Church, so often I use the adjective *unhurried*. Take *unhurried* time with God. Hence, the name of this book, *Unhurried Time With God*.

Finally, be fully present. During this time with the Lord, as much as you can, *be all there!*

This is difficult. If you are like me, my mind tends to wander, about anything and everything. I have learned not to berate myself when this happens. God is not a harsh taskmaster. He's my Papa! He's easy to live with. I simply smile to myself and thank the Lord for bringing me back.

One thing that may help you to be fully present is to pray out loud and read the Bible out loud. This is not always possible, but often it is. The more attentive you are, the more engaged you are, the more you will enjoy this time and the more you will benefit from this time.

As much as possible, be all there. Come to God, not with part of you but with all of you. Remember that you are in the presence of Almighty God. *Enter his presence.*

Other heart attitudes could be discussed, but here are six vital perspectives to keep in mind when you meet with the Lord. They will make all the difference.

1. Come to God not to learn theology, but to meet God.

2. Come to God not for information, but for transformation.

3. Come to God not out of spiritual pride, but out of profound humility.

4. Come to God not out of discipline and duty, but out of love.

5. Come to God not with a hurried spirit, but with an unhurried spirit.

6. Come to God not with part of you, but with all of you.

PART III

DIVING DEEPER

CHAPTER TEN

ELEMENTS

———————

There are countless ways of meeting with God. As I previously mentioned, where and how you meet with God is personal – there is no one way this should look, no one method better than others.

In this chapter I want to elaborate on some, though not all, of the elements involved in meeting with God. Specifically, I will dig deeper into the following nine elements:

1. The Bible
2. Prayer and the Bible
3. Singing to God
4. Thanksgiving
5. Confession
6. Petition: Ask for Yourself
7. Intercession: Ask for Others
8. Listening Prayer
9. Bible Memory

Any elements excluded from this list are not unimportant, or less important, than those I've chosen to discuss here. These, however, represent those I have personally found to be the most influential in my faith.

THE BIBLE

Consider the vitality and the power and the impact of the Bible:

> For the word of God is living and active. Sharper than any double-edged sword, it penetrates even to dividing soul and spirit, joints and marrow; it judges the thoughts and attitudes of the heart. (Hebrews 4:12)

First of all, the Bible is *alive*. If you come to the Bible with an open and humble heart, God will speak to you. God will meet you. This is not a dry, dusty, theological tome. This is not a book of abstract theological law. It is the living Word of God!

Martin Luther once wrote: "The Bible is alive; it speaks to me; it has feet, it runs after me; it has hands, it lays hold of me."

Whatever the Bible says, God says. When you open the Bible, expect to meet God. Expect to hear from God. Expect to encounter God. The biographer of the singer Rich Mullins writes of this encounter:

For Rich, the Bible was central. In his pursuit of biblical literacy, he gained more than biblical knowledge; he gained access into the presence of God. Rich understood that the reason we read the Bible at all is not to understand God but to encounter him. Rich once said, "I don't think you read the Bible to know truth. I think you read the Bible to find God, that we encounter him there. Paul says that the Scriptures are God's breath and I kind of go, 'Wow, so let's breathe this as deeply as possible.'" (Smith, *Rich Mullins*, 36.)

When Hebrews 4 talks about soul and spirit, joints and marrow, the point is not to give lessons in psychology or anatomy, but to say that no part of us is immune from God's scalpel. The Bible penetrates the impenetrable and extricates the inextricable.

All about us there is an endless flood of words, and most of these words are shallow and superficial words. But not God's words! These words are the most penetrating words in the universe. The Bible exposes who we really are. The Bible reveals our blind spots. The Bible even uncovers our secret motives. *God's Word penetrates.*

Rich Mullins reflects on the Bible:

The Bible is not a book for the faint of heart – it is a book full of all the greed and glory and violence and tenderness and sex and betrayal that befits mankind. It is not the collection of pretty little anecdotes mouthed by pious church mice – it does not so much nibble at our shoe leather as it cuts to the heart and splits the marrow from the bone. It does not give us answers fitted to our small-minded questions, but truth that goes beyond what we even know to ask. (Smith, *Rich Mullins,* 37)

The Bible is a priceless treasure, but how do we practically get into the Bible? One way is to read fairly quickly through the Bible. We could call this overview reading. Simply go to Genesis 1 and read through the Bible. Or go to Matthew 1 and read through the New Testament. By reading large chunks of Scripture you get the grand sweep of God's revelation. You get the big picture.

One excellent tool for reading the entire Bible is the One-Year Bible, which comes in several translations. The One-Year Bible includes, for each day of the year, an Old Testament passage, a New Testament passage, a passage from Psalms and a small passage from Proverbs. By reading 20 minutes a day, you cover the Bible in one year. This tool can be more interesting than just reading straight through the Bible because you have four different passages each day.

Since the Bible is inspired by God and profitable for our spiritual lives, it is a good thing to get regular exposure to every chapter in the Bible. Overview reading, or reading large chunks of the Bible, ensures that you get regular exposure to all of Scripture.

On the other hand, the downside of overview reading is that you may go so fast through the Bible that you fail to savor the treasures in each verse or paragraph. So a second approach to the Bible is to read it slowly, just a few verses a day. Maybe a paragraph. After all, the point is not that you get through the Bible, but that the Bible gets through you.

Psalm 119, the longest chapter in the Bible and the chapter focused entirely on the glories of God's Word, often speaks of this approach as meditating on Scripture: "I will meditate on your precepts and fix my eyes on your ways" (119:15). We don't just read the Bible, but we meditate on it. We ponder. We reflect. We pray through it. We chew on it like a dog chews on a bone.

Ignatius of Loyola encourages us to use all of our senses in Bible study. Smell the sea. Hear the lap of water along the shore. See the crowd. Feel the sun on your head and the hunger pangs in your stomach. Taste the salt in the air. Touch the hem of his garment.

George Müller, the renowned British pastor who saw God provide for thousands of orphans through prayer alone, said that meditation of Scripture was absolutely vital to him. He said that the first thing that he did every day was to begin meditating on the Word of God. He would search every verse, not for the sake of public ministry, but to obtain food for his own soul. As he was meditating on the Scripture, invariably this would lead to confession or thanksgiving or intercession or petition, so that meditating on the Bible led almost immediately to prayer.

In addition to overview reading and meditating, a third approach could be called inductive Bible study, which means you carefully study through a book of the Bible and derive truths from the book. The premium is not on speed, but on careful observation of what's in the text, alert interpretation of what the text means and then humble application of the text to your life.

Inductive Bible study overlaps a lot with meditation, but perhaps there's an academic nuance with inductive Bible study. Often you take lots of notes and consult several translations. Perhaps you utilize reference tools and look up words. You pore over the text, noticing everything you can.

You consider the literary genre – is this narrative or wisdom literature or poetry or Gospel or a letter or a parable or apocalyptic literature? What difference does it make? You pepper the text with questions: Who? What? Where? Why? How? You especially keep in mind the basic question: What is the point of this passage? Why did God include it?

You certainly consider the context. In Bible study, context is king. What happens before and after the passage? What is the flow of thought in the passage?

You let Scripture interpret Scripture. When you encounter a difficult or unclear passage, interpret it in light of clear passages in the rest of the Bible. The clear interprets the unclear.

With inductive study you need to be aware of *good* resources. Start with the Bible alone, not books by man. But at some point in inductive Bible study, you might consult a study Bible (a Bible with notes at the bottom, such as the ESV Study Bible or the NIV Study Bible, both of which are superb) or a Bible dictionary or a concordance.

This third approach, inductive Bible study, may seem complicated. Let me be simpler. Take a passage of the Bible and read through it several times. See if you can summarize it in your own words. Then ask a few questions: What do I learn about man? What do I learn about God? What is one specific thing that God is calling me to obey?

Another tool for inductive Bible study is the acronym SPECK:

> S – Sin
> P – Promise
> E – Example
> C – Command
> K – Knowledge

Is there a *sin* to acknowledge?

Is there a *promise* to claim?

Is there an *example* to follow?

Is there a *command* to obey?

Is there *knowledge* about God or yourself to embrace?

Two general books that I recommend are *How to Read the Bible for All Its Worth* by Douglas Stuart and Gordon Fee and *Hard Sayings of the Bible,* edited by F. F. Bruce. *How to Read the Bible for All Its Worth* is the best book I know for learning how to approach the Bible. This is a valuable book regardless if you do overview reading, meditative reading or inductive study. (I might note that as much as I love this book, I do not find their chapter on translations to be cogent. I much prefer the ESV as my basic Bible, rather than the NIV that they recommend.)

Hard Sayings of the Bible is different. The editors give a brief discussion of the difficult passages in the Bible. Both of these books are invaluable.

Let me clarify: These three approaches – overview reading, meditating, inductive Bible studying – are not exclusive. There is overlap and you can do some of each. Each approach has its strengths. In a given season of your spiritual life, God may lead you to emphasize one approach. But if I had to choose only one approach as my bread and butter, it would be to slowly meditate through Scripture.

Regardless of your approach, read prayerfully. Don't so much read the Bible as pray the Bible. Read with humility. Read to obey. Read more for transformation than for information. And especially, read to meet God.

Prayer and the Bible

In Ephesians 3:14 Paul writes, "For this reason I bow my knees before the Father." *For this reason.* For what reason?

Because of all that Paul has just written about in Ephesians 1-3, all that God has done for us in Christ Jesus, all that God has revealed to us of his grace and glory, for *that* reason, Paul prays for the Ephesian Christians.

When God reveals his glory to us, his grace to us, his will for us, it is only natural that we respond in prayer. That's why the Bible and prayer go together.

Our Bible reading shapes and infuses our prayer. Conversely, our prayer completes and enriches our Bible reading. They go together.

The Word of God is critical to prayer, just as prayer is critical to the Word of God. The Word shows us how to pray; prayer enables us to understand the Word. The Word shows us who

God is; prayer ushers us into God's presence. Reading the Word shapes our praying; our praying gives life to reading the Word.

Prayer and the Word of God go together. What God has joined together let no man separate.

When you read the Bible pray as you read it. Pray for wisdom, for insight, for understanding, for application. Agree with the Scripture. "Yes, Lord, make it so." "Oh yes, Lord. You can do it." "Forgive me, Lord."

You are not merely reading a book of theology, truths about God. You are reading God's Word, which is alive and active and empowered by the Holy Spirit. You are reading love letters from your Father. You are meeting with God. You ask God to speak to you through his Word and then you in turn pour out your heart to God. This is conversation. This is dialogue. *This is prayer.*

Pray your way through Scripture.

Eugene Peterson, the translator of *The Message,* noted:

> The Scriptures, read and prayed, are our primary and normative access to God as he reveals himself to us. The Scriptures are our listening post for learning the language of the soul, the ways God speaks to us; they also provide the vocabulary and grammar that are appropriate for us as we in our turn speak

to God. Prayer detached from Scripture, from listening to God, disconnected from God's words to us, short-circuits the relational language that is prayer. Christians acquire this personal and relational practice of prayer primarily (although not exclusively) under the shaping influence of the Psalms and Jesus. (*Eat This Book*, p. 104)

Andrew Murray, the South African pastor and writer, put it more succinctly:

Prayer and the Word of God are inseparable, and should always go together in the quiet time of the inner chamber. This really gives prayer its power, that I take God's thoughts from his Word and present them before him. How indispensable God's Word is for all true prayer.

Singing to God

Singing is one of the most powerful forms of praise and yet singing is often neglected as a rich part of meeting with God.

Perhaps you feel uncomfortable with singing to God. Maybe you don't recognize or fully agree with the importance of worshipping him in song. Consider this.

Have you ever been driving in your car listening to the radio and heard a song that completely transformed your mood?

Maybe it made you somber and reflective, when a moment before you had felt content. Or perhaps it instantly lifted your mood and energy when before you felt fatigued or down.

Most would agree that music can set the tone of a room. Whether it be the music playing as a bride walks down the aisle towards her waiting groom, or the song you choose to give that last bit of effort in a workout, or the song you sing at the top of your lungs on a road trip with your best friends. The power of music is undeniable.

If the power of music is so pervasive in our daily lives, how much more powerful is it when used for its original purpose: to worship the Father in Heaven? God created music as a tool for us to praise him. When we use music for that purpose, how much deeper can we feel the presence of God. How much richer does our time with him become.

Singing is a prominent form of praise throughout the Bible, but nowhere is singing as prominent as it is in the Psalms. The very word *Psalms* means *Songs*. These are the songs of Israel, meant to be sung to God. We have the lyrics but not the music.

In the Book of Psalms there are over a hundred references to the word *sing* or the word *song*. For example *(emphasis added)*:

But let all who take refuge in you rejoice,
Let them ever *sing* for joy.
Psalm 5:11a

I will *sing* praise to your name, O Most High.
Psalm 9:2b

Sing praises to the Lord, O you his saints.
Psalm 30:4a

But I will *sing* of your strength;
I will *sing* aloud of your steadfast love in the
morning.
Psalm 59:16a,b

Oh *sing* to the Lord a new *song*;
Sing to the Lord, all the earth!
Sing to the Lord, bless his name;
Tell of his salvation from day to day.
Psalm 96:1-2

Oh *sing* to the Lord a new *song*,
For he has done marvelous things!
Psalm 98:1a

Serve the Lord with gladness!
Come into his presence with *singing!*
Psalm 100:2

Why does singing matter so much to God?

What else expresses the heart so deeply? What else allows us to express our love to God so powerfully?

God created us to sing – even those of us who cannot sing a note! To be more accurate: God created us to sing to *him*. He has implanted a "singing gene" into our souls. This "singing gene" is not the *ability* to sing, but the *desire* to sing to God.

We yearn to sing to God. You may have suppressed this yearning, but it is there. There is no need to deprive yourself any longer of this exhilarating pleasure when you connect with God in a deeply intimate way.

Sometimes, when we are singing to God as a church family, there is something about the combination of words and music and praise band and singers and heartfelt voices that is inexpressibly moving, to the point that the beauty and joy is almost painful to me. The atmosphere is electric, charged with the glory and grandeur of God. It is powerful!

What is it about singing to God that is so powerful? I am not sure. There is a mystery to music that transcends logic. It is a mystery born in the heart of God, who is the Creator of music and the Master Musician.

The godly Jim Elliot, who would eventually give his life for Christ in the Amazon jungle, wrote in his prayer journal about singing:

Enjoyed the truth of singing "psalms and hymns and spiritual songs" this morning. Found my prayer list so unstimulating to real prayer that I laid it aside and took the Inter-Varsity Hymnal and sang aloud with much heart-warming such songs as seemed to fit my need. This is as decidedly a means of grace as anything given by God to His people, but how little we use it! (*Shadow of the Almighty*, p. 111)

Music is powerful! It's emotional! It's passionate!

Music is the language of love.

At times, in our worship, we feel so deeply, that only singing can express what we feel inside. Just *saying* the words won't do. We've got to sing them!

Augustine felt that when we sing we pray twice – once with words and once at another level in the music of the heart.

Music is a gift. A gift from God. So sing those songs. Those God songs. Those songs of love and praise and wonder. Sing with all your heart! Sing aloud! Sing to God! For when you sing to God your whole view of God is transformed and exalted and your heart is moved to love him more.

THANKSGIVING

The Bible repeatedly calls us to give thanks to God. For

example, 1 Thessalonians 5:18 tells us: "Give thanks in all circumstances; for this is the will of God in Christ Jesus for you."

Why is this so important to God? Why does *my* gratitude matter to the sovereign and infinite God who created the galaxies?

First of all, God deserves our gratitude. It's only right that we thank him. Everything good in our lives is a gift from God. Paul asks, "What do you have that you did not receive?" (1 Corinthians 4:7). The answer? Nothing. Nothing at all. God has been so good to us.

Secondly, we thank God because we have a deep need to express gratitude. To say thank you to God is part of the image of God in us. We are hard-wired as image bearers to give thanks to God. Down deep we know that God has been good to us and we ought to give thanks.

It has been pointed out that the problem with atheism is that the atheist has no one to thank when he feels grateful for life's good things. Imagine an atheist who has a 25-year-old son who escapes the World Trade Center on September 11, 2001. Everything in him wants to thank God, but he has denied to himself that God even exists.

Thirdly, gratitude is important because gratitude shows faith in God. Every time we say thank you to God we express our faith. Every prayer of thanksgiving expresses our faith that God exists and that he is good and that he has been good to us. This is why Jesus says to the healed leper, who returns to say thank you, *"You faith has made you well."* Every prayer of gratitude shows faith.

In *True Spirituality* Francis Schaeffer wrote, "A quiet disposition and heart giving thanks at any given moment is the real test of the extent to which we love God at that moment."

Find yourself, every day, thanking God for his blessings. Thank him for his outrageous love for you. Thank him that he has forgiven all your sins. Thank him that you are safe in him forever. Thank him that he will never leave you or forsake you.

Thank him for a Savior. Thank him for the incarnation. Thank him for the perfect life and matchless teachings of Jesus. Thank him for a bloody cross. Thank him for the resurrection.

Thank him for the Spirit inside you and for all the ministries of the Spirit. Thank him for his power. Thank him for answered prayer. Thank him for unanswered prayer.

Thank him for the Bible in your own language.

Thank him for food each day and a warm place to stay. Thank him for blue sky and brilliant moon. Thank him for people who care about you.

Thank him for the struggles of life and how he redeems those struggles. Thank him for the glory to come, glory that is far beyond your sufferings.

O give thanks to the Lord! For he is good!

Fourthly, gratitude builds faith. Giving thanks to God not only *expresses* faith but it also *builds* faith. Every day when we thank God for his marvelous blessings and gifts to us, we are reminded of God's goodness, God's love of us, God's fatherly care for us, God's grace to us, God's provision for us. We are reminded of God's faithfulness in the past and we are more likely to trust him for our future.

Prayers of thanksgiving build faith.

Finally, gratitude is vital because grateful people are happy people. When we give thanks to God, our spirits are brightened. Our gaze is lifted from what we lack to what we have. We are more content and grateful and trusting. Clouds in our soul begin to break up and sunshine begins to break through.

A thankful spirit fosters joy, peace and contentment and it erodes jealousy, bitterness and gloom.

Lewis Smedes, at the end of his life, wrote a remarkable statement about gratitude:

> I learned long ago that if anything can be better than

getting a gift, it is the gratitude we feel for getting it. There is no other pleasure to compare with it – not sex, not winning a lottery, not hearing lovely music, not seeing stunning mountain peaks, nothing. Gratitude beats them all. I have never met a grateful person who was an unhappy person. And, for that matter, I have never met a grateful person who was a bad person. *(My God and I, a Spiritual Memoir)*

The happiest people on earth are the grateful people.

Gordon MacDonald was referring to the passage in Luke 17, when nine of ten lepers did not go back to Jesus to thank him for healing them, and he remarked:

The thankful spirit – the intent beneath the words – is the result of continuous discipline, because gratefulness isn't a natural or instinctive thing for most of us. Perhaps the fact that nine of the ten never came back illustrates this. Thankfulness is a learned transaction, and it comes with the realization that I neither deserve nor am entitled to blessings. At best, I am a graced recipient of all I have and am.

… Thomas Kelly [once wrote]:

We pray for the big things and forget to give thanks for the ordinary, small (and yet really not small) gifts. How can God entrust great

> things to one who will not thankfully receive
> from Him the little things? (MacDonald, *A
> Resilient Life, 134)*

Ambrose, the early church father who had such impact on Augustine, put it bluntly: "No duty is more urgent than that of returning thanks."

In light of these five reasons, it is not surprising that Hans Selye, who did the seminal research on stress, found that the single most critical emotion for mental health was gratitude. It is no wonder that an all-wise Father tells us to give thanks in everything.

Gratitude matters. It matters to God. It matters to us. It matters a lot.

CONFESSION

There is power in confession. To confess our sins to God is to pull the drain plug on guilt. All our sin and guilt swooshes down the drain, vanishing forever in God's grace.

When we confess our sin, we simply agree with God about our sin. "Lord, I was dishonest with Bob." "Father, forgive me for losing my temper with Tommy." "O God, forgive my pride. I didn't need to brag about my job with those people."

Frederick Buechner puts the matter poignantly in *Wishful*

Thinking: A Theological ABC: "To confess your sins to God is not to tell him anything he doesn't already know. Until you confess them, however, they are the abyss between you. When you confess them, they become the bridge."

I find the same thing happens in my marriage. If I am unkind or insensitive with Gayle, we may still be married, but there is now a barrier between us. We are connected in a legal and judicial sense, but we are not connected in a relational and fellowship sense. But when I apologize to Gayle, everything changes. Our closeness and oneness is restored. There is power in confession.

God gives us a wonderful promise in 1 John 1:9: "If we confess our sins, he is faithful and just to forgive us our sins and to cleanse us from all unrighteousness."

This is the Christian bar of soap. When we confess our sin, he will restore us to full, unblemished fellowship with him.

Confession is part of prayer. We don't need to be overly introspective, but neither should we be insensitive to the Spirit's gentle convicting work. When God graciously (it is an act of grace) reminds us of our sin, then immediately and sincerely confess it to God and experience the fresh joy of his cleansing grace.

In one sense, a legal and judicial sense, all our sin has already been forgiven. All our sin was nailed to the cross and we are under no condemnation (Romans 8:1).

But there is another sense, a relational and fellowship sense, that our relationship with God is hindered by our sin. There is a barrier between us until we confess our sin to God. This is the point of 1 John 1:9.

PETITION: ASK FOR YOURSELF

It is amazing how frequently, and how emphatically, the Bible tells us to bring our prayer requests to the Father. Just a few examples:

> *Ask*, and it will be given to you; *seek*, and you will find; *knock*, and it will be opened to you. For everyone who *asks* receives, and the one who *seeks* finds, and to the one who *knocks* it will be opened (Matthew 7:7-8, *emphasis added*).

> Whatever you *ask* in my name, this I will do, that the Father may be glorified in the Son. If you *ask* me anything in my name, I will do it (John 14:13-14, *emphasis added*).

> Until now you have *asked* nothing in my name. *Ask*, and you will receive, that your joy may be full (John 16:24, *emphasis added*).

> You do not have, because you do not *ask* (James 4:2b, *emphasis added*).

Over and over again: Ask! Ask! Ask! Such emphasis!

God wants us to ask. But what do we ask for? Whatever is in your heart. Whatever you care about. Whatever you need. Whatever you are burdened about. Ask!

Sometimes we ask things for other people, but we may hesitate to pray for ourselves. It feels a bit self-centered.

But Jesus wants us to pray for our own needs. Look at your prayer requests, not as an expression of self-centeredness but as an expression of dependence on God. When we bring our requests to God, whether for others or for ourselves, we are implicitly saying to God: "Lord, I need you. Lord, I am dependent upon you. Lord, you care about my needs. Lord, you have the power to meet my needs. Lord, I trust you."

Asking God for things is a matter of dependence, not selfishness. Asking things for ourselves expresses faith and humility and dependence. It is the very opposite of a proud, self-reliant independence.

Augustine said, "God is more anxious to bestow his blessings on us than we are to receive them."

And Richard Foster, in his book *Prayer*, wrote: "The Cambridge professor Herbert Farmer reminds us that 'if prayer is the heart of religion, then petition is the heart of prayer.' Without Petitionary Prayer we have a truncated prayer life. May I remind us all once again how very much God delights in our asking, looking for an excuse to give."

So ask! Ask frequently! Ask freely! Ask for yourself! Ask for whatever you need! Even ask for your wants! Ask!

You are loved intensely by your heavenly Father and he wants you to bring all your requests to him.

INTERCESSION: ASK FOR OTHERS

You've got to love Epaphras. He is from the city of Colossae, but he is now with Paul in Rome. Yet his heart is still in Colossae, with his people. So he prays for them. And how he does pray! "Epaphras, who is one of you, a servant of Christ Jesus, greets you, always struggling on your behalf in his prayers, that you may stand mature and fully assured in all the will of God" (Colossians 4:12).

He *struggles* in prayer. What does it mean to struggle in prayer? I'm not completely sure, but I am sure what it is not. It is not tepid prayer, lifeless prayer, soulless prayer or mechanical prayer. No, Epaphras *struggles* in prayer for his people. He goes to battle! He storms the gates! He attacks the hill! His prayer has heart! Life! Passion!

> *O God! Please intervene! You've just got to!*
> *Protect them! Deliver them! Rescue them!*

Moreover, not only does Epaphras struggle in prayer for

them, he is *always* struggling in prayer for them. Not just on rare occasions but continually, day in and day out.

And what does he pray? That the Colossians would stand mature with God, right in the middle of God's will, fully assured of where they stand with God. Epaphras is praying for a healthy and strong spiritual life, so that they would be all that God wanted them to be.

Paul was also an intercessor. For example, in Romans 1 he writes: "For God is my witness, whom I serve with my spirit in the gospel of his Son, that without ceasing I mention you always in my prayers" (1:9-10a).

Paul prays for the believers in Rome. Not only does Paul pray for them, but he prays for them *constantly*, without ceasing. And not only does he pray for them constantly but he *tells* them that he prays for them constantly. Paul must have known that these believers, whom he had never met, would be encouraged from the depths of their hearts, to know that the Apostle Paul was regularly praying for them.

In the fall of 1972, I met John Lodwick, a fellow freshman at Rice University. Little did I know that John and I would become fast friends and room together for the next eight years, through college and graduate school.

Sometime after meeting John I began praying for him every day. Perhaps it was in the first weeks or in the first months after meeting him. I no longer remember. But I began praying for him every day. I have done that now for over 47 years and I will continue to pray for John for the rest of my years on earth.

John is a close friend and regularly praying for him is the single most important thing I can do for him.

Moreover, not only do I pray for John daily but John prays for me. I know he does. And from time to time, he tells me that he prays for me daily. I already know it but still it is good to hear it afresh, "I'm praying for you daily."

Just as Paul prayed continually for the Christians at Rome and told them he did, and just as John Lodwick prays continually for me and tells me he does, let's pray continually for the people God puts on our hearts. And let's tell them we are praying for them. They will be encouraged from the depths of their hearts.

For intercession is an act of love. It is an act of sacrificial love. If you are a follower of Jesus and you care about a person, then you pray for that person. Dietrich Bonhoeffer wrote: "A Christian fellowship lives and exists by the intercession of its members for one another, or it collapses" (*Life Together*, p. 86).

Paul prayed continually for fellow believers because he knew that prayer was the real work of ministry. Prayer was not a preliminary activity or an optional activity to Paul. Prayer was the main thing he did.

Because prayer accesses the power of God. Prayer accesses the heart of God. Prayer accesses the mind of God.

Prayer is not you and *your* resources reaching out to help someone. Prayer is you and *God's* resources reaching out to help someone.

What's bigger than that? What's grander than that? What's higher than that?

Prayer is important. It is vitally important. But it is not easy. It is a sacrifice. It takes time. It takes energy. It takes heart. If you pour your heart out for someone, you bleed inside. John Henry Jowett once wrote: "Prayer is a sacrifice, a bleeding sacrifice."

Furthermore, prayer is quite often unseen, unnoticed, unapplauded and unappreciated. But that's OK. God sees our prayer and God loves our prayer. For prayer is the main work of ministry.

Do you intercede for the people in your life? Do you frequently and fervently call out to God for your family, your friends, your loved ones, your church, the lost?

Lives are changed because of intercessors. History is changed because of intercessors. Walter Wink put it this way: "History belongs to the intercessors."

LISTENING PRAYER

The classic passage on listening prayer is the fascinating scene in 1 Samuel 3 when God speaks to the young Samuel and he doesn't know that it is God speaking.

The very first verse of the chapter is telling: "Now the boy Samuel was ministering to the LORD in the presence of Eli. And the word of the LORD was rare in those days; there was no frequent vision." The clear implication: The voice of God is not always infrequent. The word of the Lord is not always rare. This was an exceptional time because of the people's sin. Normally, it was common for God to speak.

The story continues:

> One night Eli, whose eyes were becoming so weak that he could barely see, was lying down in his usual place. The lamp of God had not yet gone out, and Samuel was lying down in the house of the Lord, where the ark of God was.
>
> Then the Lord called Samuel. Samuel answered, "Here I am." And he ran to Eli and said, "Here I am; you called me." But Eli said, "I did not call; go back and lie down." So he went and lay down.
>
> Again the Lord called, "Samuel!" And Samuel got up and went to Eli and said, "Here I am; you called me." "My son," Eli said, "I did not call; go back and lie

down." Now Samuel did not yet know the Lord: The word of the Lord had not yet been revealed to him.

A third time the Lord called, "Samuel!" And Samuel got up and went to Eli and said, "Here I am; you called me." Then Eli realized that the Lord was calling the boy. So Eli told Samuel, "Go and lie down, and if he calls you, say, 'Speak, Lord, for your servant is listening.'" So Samuel went and lay down in his place.

The Lord came and stood there, calling as at the other times, "Samuel! Samuel!" Then Samuel said, "Speak, for your servant is listening."

And the Lord said to Samuel: "See, I am about to do something in Israel that will make the ears of everyone who hears about it tingle. At that time I will carry out against Eli everything I spoke against his family—from beginning to end. For I told him that I would judge his family forever because of the sin he knew about; his sons blasphemed God, and he failed to restrain them. Therefore I swore to the house of Eli, 'The guilt of Eli's house will never be atoned for by sacrifice or offering.'" (1 Samuel 3:2-14, NIV)

God would continue to speak to Samuel for the rest of his life. No doubt Samuel got more words from God than the normal Israeli, because he was the leading prophet in the land. But did God speak to others? This is what we find all through the Bible: From Genesis to Revelation, God speaks to his people. He spoke to Adam and Eve. He spoke to Noah. He gave Abraham a special leading for his future. Jacob had a dream. Moses got a burning bush – and numerous leadings. Joseph, Deborah, Samuel, the parents of Samson, Elijah, David (so many times), Solomon, Daniel. Certainly the major and minor prophets of the Old Testament. Peter, Paul, Philip, Agabus. On and on.

The Bible is full of God speaking to his people, with impressions, leadings, dreams, visions, even an audible voice at times. God speaks, and not just to apostles and prophets. For example, in Acts 9 God gives a vision to a disciple named Ananias. It's all through the Bible. From first to last.

Is the Bible a book of exceptions? Or is the Bible a book of examples?

Samuel has a good prayer for us in 1 Samuel 3: "Speak, [Lord,] for your servant is listening" (NIV). Unfortunately, for most Christians, the mindset is *not* "Speak, Lord, for your servant is listening," *but* "Listen Lord, for your servant is speaking."

If we are going to take the Bible for our guide, and not just the tradition we grew up in or the opinion of some teacher, then we must conclude: This is the way God deals with his people. He speaks to us in all kinds of ways. Not just in Scripture, but with impressions, leadings, convictions, dreams and visions,

God is a God who speaks. God is a God who speaks to his people.

I suppose it is possible that the Bible is full of God speaking to his people in all kinds of ways, from Genesis to Revelation, and yet this is not the way God deals with us today. It is possible that the Bible is a book of exceptions. But it is extremely unlikely. The Bible itself tells us that it is a book of examples, not a book of exceptions, a book written for our instruction.

Yes the Bible is unique. It is God's authoritative written Word and it stands as judge and arbiter over all else. But if we follow the Bible, and not just give lip service to the Bible while we follow men's traditions, then we will take the biblical view: God speaks to his people in all kinds of ways. Everything must be evaluated by Scripture, but God speaks in all kinds of ways.

Down deep we know that God speaks. If he is anything, he is a God who speaks, a God who reveals, a personal and loving God. We don't follow a philosophy or a religion or a book of dry theology. We have a personal, love relationship with the living God. Of course God speaks into our lives and leads us!

The problem is that we all have seen listening prayer abused. We have heard some believer state, "God told me ..." when we were quite sure God had *not* told him that. But just because a gift can be abused does not mean there is not the legitimate example of that gift. We use our discernment, just as God tells us to. But we must not quench the Spirit. "Do not quench the Spirit. Do not despise prophecies" (1 Thessalonians 5:19-20).

One challenge with hearing from God is our lack of silence and solitude. We have far too much noise in our lives and in our heads. We seem to have an aversion to quietness and stillness. Blaise Pascal once wrote: "All of man's misery is derived from his inability to sit quietly by himself in a room alone."

If we fill our lives with noise and activity and talking, it will be difficult for us to hear the voice of God. David Brainerd, who was close to the great Puritan theologian Jonathan Edwards, once wrote: "In the silences I make in the midst of the turmoil of life I have appointments with God. From these silences I come forth with spirit refreshed, and with a renewed sense of power. I hear a voice in the silences, and become increasingly aware that it is the voice of God."

There are many churches and organizations which insist that listening prayer is not biblical. But they are inconsistent. They believe God convicts us of sin. That's God speaking. They believe we can pray Psalm 139:23-24:

> Search me, O God, and know my heart!
> Try me and know my thoughts!
> And see if there be any grievous way in me,
> and lead me in the way everlasting!

They believe God calls us to leave one job and go to another job. That's God speaking. Where does the Bible say that God speaks with conviction of sin or with calling but not in other ways? That is following man's tradition rather than biblical teaching. If we are going to take the biblical view, then we must believe that God speaks to us, not only through Scripture, but in other ways as well.

In fact, God is always speaking to us and we must be attentive to his voice at all times. Frederick Faber wrote, "There is hardly ever a complete silence in our soul. God is whispering to us well-nigh incessantly. Whenever the sounds of the world die out in the soul, or sink low, then we hear these whisperings of God. He is always whispering to us, only we do not always hear, because of the noise, hurry, and distraction which life causes as it rushes on."

Now I agree that this matter of God speaking can be difficult. "How do we know it is God's voice that I'm hearing and not just my own voice?" "Some talk so confidently of hearing God, but it is never so clear for me." "Often I ask God to speak with me and it seems I hear nothing, at least nothing that is clearly of God."

These are good questions. Honest questions. And you will get no simplistic answers from me. I wrestle with these questions also. How can we be biblical with listening prayer?

First of all, we need to believe that God speaks. Believe the

Bible. Then we might ask him to speak to us and to block out all other voices except his voice. And then we must trust that he will put things on our heart and in our mind.

Silence is important. "Be still, and know that I am God. I will be exalted among the nations, I will be exalted in the earth!" (Psalm 46:10). "For God alone my soul waits in silence" (Psalm 62:1a). And it's not just quietness in the room that we need. We also need quietness in our head.

Also, be willing to obey the Lord. David would ask God to speak to him:

> Therefore David inquired of the LORD, "Shall I go and attack these Philistines?" And the Lord said to David, "Go and attack the Philistines and save Keilah." But David's men said to him, "Behold, we are afraid here in Judah; how much more then if we go to Keilah against the armies of the Philistines?" Then David inquired of the LORD again. And the LORD answered him, "Arise, go down to Keilah, for I will give the Philistines into your hand." And David and his men went to Keilah and fought with the Philistines and brought away their livestock and struck them with a great blow. So David saved the inhabitants of Keilah. (1 Samuel 23:2-5, ESV)

David obeyed the Lord. If David had stopped obeying, then God would have stopped speaking to him. We too must inquire of the Lord: "Lord what should I do about this problem?" And we too must be ready to obey.

Also, be aware of any barriers. Sin will separate us from God and block the voice of God in our lives. Perhaps you don't *want* to hear God's voice because you're afraid of what he might say. Maybe you feel unworthy of hearing God. Perhaps you are not willing to stop talking long enough to hear God! Be aware of barriers to the voice of God.

It's important that we don't demand God to speak. He is not our servant. *We* are the servants. The main thing is just to be in God's presence and enjoy his loving presence, whether or not we hear something from God. Don't be demanding.

Humility is fitting. "This is what I think God said to me." "I believe this is what God is putting on my heart." I'd love to see more humility when it comes to listening prayer.

In the Chronicles of Narnia, Aslan says of Uncle Andrew:

> "He thinks great folly, child," said Aslan. "This world is bursting with life for these few days because the song with which I called it into life still hangs in the air and rumbles in the ground. It will not be so for long. But I cannot tell that to this old sinner, and I cannot comfort him either; he has made himself unable to hear my voice. If I spoke to him, he would hear only growling and roarings. Oh Adam's sons,

how cleverly you defend yourselves against all that might do you good! But I will give him the only gift he is still able to receive."

Do not make yourself *unable* to hear the voice of God.

Gordon MacDonald tells this anecdote:

At lunch a couple of weeks back, a man I greatly respect (age 60 this month) responds to my question, "What's God been saying to you since we were last together?" He says, "I've spent my whole life running, achieving. You know me – I've been a hammer, and everyone else has been the anvil. I've tried to fill every moment with something to do. I've always been telling God what I wanted … what I thought He should be doing. But now I'm learning that praying is as much about listening and waiting as all my previous talking. And each time I've listened, and each time I've waited, God has done something – small or large – that has left me breathless and aware of how much I've missed in all my busyness."

Beware of the busyness that blocks the voice of God.

Along these lines, A.W. Tozer gives strong testimony of how powerful this listening prayer can be:

When I am praying the most eloquently, I am getting the least accomplished in my prayer life. But when I

stop getting eloquent and give God less theology and
shut up and just gaze upward and wait for God to
speak to my heart he speaks with such power that I
have to grab a pencil and a notebook and take notes
on what God is saying to my heart.

Or there's this line from Oswald Chambers, the author of *My
Utmost for His Highest,* "Get into the habit of saying, 'Speak,
Lord,' and life will become a romance … one great romance, a
glorious opportunity for seeing marvelous things all the time."

I can tell you that from my personal experience it is a sweet
and rich time to be silent before the Lord, to be open to what
he puts on your heart and in your mind, to ask him a question,
and then be still and listen. It is one thing to hear a message
from a Christian friend, but it is a much deeper thing to hear
a message from God, for God to speak deeply into your soul
about his love for you, about what you should focus on.

Most days, I will ask the Lord something like this, "Is there
anything that I need to hear from you today?" Then I will be
quiet, in both voice and mind, and perhaps I will sense an
impression like this from the Lord: "Jeff, you need to be more
attentive to Gayle today." Or, "Jeff, this ministry event is not
about you. It is all about Jesus." Or, "Jeff, today you just need
to focus on loving me and enjoying me." These may not seem
like profound or life-changing messages, but they are heart
changing when they come from the Father.

If listening prayer is not a regular part of your prayer life, what do you do? Here are two prayers that might resonate with your soul. The first is from Richard Foster, from his superb book on prayer:

> My Lord and my God, listening is hard for me. I do not exactly mean hard, for I understand that this is a matter of receiving rather than trying. What I mean is that I am so action oriented, so product driven, that doing is easier for me than being. I need your help if I am to be still and listen. I would like to try. I would like to learn how to sink down into the light of your presence until I can become comfortable in that posture. Help me to try now. Thank you. Amen.
> (Foster, *Prayer,* 165)

The second prayer comes from A.W. Tozer:

> Lord, teach me to listen. The times are noisy and my ears are weary with the thousand raucous sounds which continuously assault them … let me hear You speaking in my heart. Let me get used to the sound of Your voice, that its tones may be familiar when the sounds of earth die away and the only sound will be the music of your speaking voice. Amen.

Michael Mickan is a close friend who has mentored me in listening prayer. He once gave me these suggestions:

Admit right from the start that you are not in control and you are surrendering any desire for that to him. It's God's prerogative when and how he chooses to speak, so listening isn't so much about what God says as your attitude of waiting on him like a faithful servant, ready to obey what his master says.

Ask the Holy Spirit repeatedly to guide you. Admit that you'll mess it up if you try to do this right and that you entrust yourself to the Holy Spirit's lead. God will speak in all kinds of ways and at different times, and just asking the Holy Spirit to guide you in listening is crucial so that you don't focus on some "posture" or performance-oriented method. Again, this is about an attitude of listening rather than method designed to elicit a response from the Lord.

Quiet your mind. We can be still on the outside and busy on the inside. Quiet your mind and just *be* before the Lord. Focus on him. Take a posture of quiet waiting on the Lord.

Be ready to respond if the Lord says something to you. If you already have decided what you will and will not do before you listen, what's the point of listening?

While you're going through your time with God, or preparing your sermon, or doing anything throughout the day, repeatedly stop yourself and ask "Lord, is there anything you want to say about this?" Then actually wait to see if the Lord has anything to say. Over time I doubt you will have to mentally go through this exercise, you'll most likely just *be* in this attitude, which is what you're aiming for.

Hold on to what you *hear* lightly. Be prepared to *hear* wrongly. Between our brokenness, spiritual interference, and the condition of sin in this world, you won't always hear correctly. Sometimes it's just what you might be saying to yourself. Be ready to trash whatever you thought you heard if it doesn't turn out. Your willingness to move forward even in the face of your error is an act of submission. It's why I never say "The Lord said…" but always say something to the effect of "I believe the Lord might be saying…" or "I think the Lord might be leading that…." It's not a lack of confidence, just a recognition of brokenness.

Bible Memory

One of the very best things you can do for your relationship with God, for your *life,* all of life, is to hide God's Word in your heart. Memorize important verses! Learn them. Go over them. Meditate on them. Say them aloud to yourself. Chew on them.

Whenever we memorize a verse or a passage, we are implanting that verse deeply in our soul, where God can use it to encourage us, guide us and transform us.

Moreover, when we fill our mind with God's mind by memorizing passages, we have God's truths at our fingertips, ready to use in any situation, a sword ready for battle. Think of Jesus in Matthew 4:1-11 with the temptation account. Three times Satan came at him to devour his soul and three times Jesus quoted a verse from the Bible and stood upon the truth of that verse.

When I was a new Christian, Randy Youngling, an upper classman, discipled me and had me memorize the 60 verses in the Navigators' Topical Memory System, or TMS. (I highly recommend this plan. It has been the time-tested gold standard for decades. Google it to find the verses or order the kit.) I learned the TMS verses and went on to learn other vital verses. These passages have proven to be an invaluable source of wisdom and comfort and peace and warning for over 40 years. They have become part of my heart, part of my mind, part of my soul.

When I have been fearful, I've pulled out John 14:1: "Do not let your heart be troubled; believe in God, believe also in me."

When I've been perplexed, I've gone to Proverbs 3:5-6: "Trust in the Lord with all your heart / And do not lean on your own understanding. / In all your ways acknowledge him, /

And he will make your paths straight."

When I've been anxious, I've reminded myself of Philippians 4:6-7: "Be anxious for nothing, but in everything by prayer and supplication with thanksgiving let your requests be made known to God. And the peace of God, which surpasses all comprehension, will guard your hearts and your minds in Christ Jesus" (NKJV).

When I've felt attacked, I've recited 1 John 4:4: "... he who is in you is greater than he who is in the world."

When I've felt guilty, I've claimed Romans 8:1: "Therefore there is now no condemnation for those who are in Christ Jesus."

When I've been convicted of sin, I've turned to 1 John 1:9: "If we confess our sins, he is faithful and righteous to forgive us our sins and to cleanse us from all unrighteousness."

Charles Swindoll, leading pastor and writer, is most emphatic on Bible memory: "I know of no other single practice in the Christian life more rewarding, practically speaking, than memorizing Scripture. That's right. No other single discipline is more useful and rewarding than this. No other single exercise pays greater spiritual dividends!" (Insight for Living, "How to Make Scripture Stick")

A few years ago I prayerfully chose 52 verses in the Bible to memorize. I chose these verses for our congregation and I encouraged them to memorize one a week for 52 weeks. The list is somewhat arbitrary, but I selected these verses on the basis of how important they are and how practical they are for the daily spiritual life. Here is my list *(this list is also included in the appendix for reference as well)*:

1. **Joshua 1:8**

   This Book of the Law shall not depart from your mouth, but you shall meditate on it day and night, so that you may be careful to do according to all that is written in it. For then you will make your way prosperous, and then you will have good success.

2. **Psalm 103:11-12**

   For as high as the heavens are above the earth,
       so great is his steadfast love toward those who fear him;
   as far as the east is from the west,
       so far does he remove our transgressions from us.

3. **Proverbs 3:5-6**

   Trust in the LORD with all your heart,
       and do not lean on your own understanding
   In all your ways acknowledge him,
       and he will make straight your paths.

4. **Isaiah 53:6**

   All we like sheep have gone astray;

we have turned—every one—to his own way;
and the LORD has laid on him
the iniquity of us all.

5. Jeremiah 9:23-24

Thus says the LORD: "Let not the wise man boast in his wisdom, let not the mighty man boast in his might, let not the rich man boast in his riches, but let him who boasts boast in this, that he understands and knows me, that I am the LORD who practices steadfast love, justice, and righteousness in the earth. For in these things I delight, declares the LORD."

6. Matthew 4:19

And he said to them, "Follow me, and I will make you fishers of men."

7. Matthew 11:28

Come to me, all who labor and are heavy laden, and I will give you rest.

8. Matthew 22:37-39

And he said to him, "You shall love the Lord your God with all your heart and with all your soul and with all your mind. This is the great and first commandment. And a second is like it: You shall love your neighbor as yourself."

9. **Matthew 23:12**

Whoever exalts himself will be humbled, and whoever humbles himself will be exalted.

10. **Matthew 28:18-20**

And Jesus came and said to them, "All authority in heaven and on earth has been given to me. Go therefore and make disciples of all nations, baptizing them in the name of the Father and of the Son and of the Holy Spirit, teaching them to observe all that I have commanded you. And behold, I am with you always, to the end of the age."

11. **Mark 10:45**

For even the Son of Man came not to be served but to serve, and to give his life as a ransom for many.

12. **Luke 9:23**

And he said to all, "If anyone would come after me, let him deny himself and take up his cross daily and follow me."

13. **John 1:1**

In the beginning was the Word, and the Word was with God, and the Word was God.

14. **John 1:12**

But to all who did receive him, who believed in his name, he gave the right to become children of God.

15. John 1:14

And the Word became flesh and dwelt among us, and we have seen his glory, glory as of the only Son from the Father, full of grace and truth.

16. John 3:16

For God so loved the world, that he gave his only Son, that whoever believes in him should not perish but have eternal life.

17. John 8:31-32

So Jesus said to the Jews who had believed him, "If you abide in my word, you are truly my disciples, and you will know the truth, and the truth will set you free."

18. John 13:35

By this all people will know that you are my disciples, if you have love for one another.

19. John 14:1

Let not your hearts be troubled. Believe in God; believe also in me.

20. John 14:6

Jesus said to him, "I am the way, and the truth, and the life. No one comes to the Father except through me."

21. John 14:21

Whoever has my commandments and keeps them, he it is who loves me. And he who loves me will be loved by my Father, and I will love him and manifest myself to him.

22. Acts 1:8

But you will receive power when the Holy Spirit has come upon you, and you will be my witnesses in Jerusalem and in all Judea and Samaria, and to the end of the earth.

23. Acts 16:31

And they said, "Believe in the Lord Jesus, and you will be saved, you and your household."

24. Romans 1:16

For I am not ashamed of the gospel, for it is the power of God for salvation to everyone who believes, to the Jew first and also to the Greek.

25. Romans 3:23

For all have sinned and fall short of the glory of God.

26. Romans 3:25-26

Whom God put forward as a propitiation by his blood, to be received by faith. This was to show God's righteousness, because in his divine forbearance he had passed over former sins. It was to show his righteousness

at the present time, so that he might be just and the
justifier of the one who has faith in Jesus.

27. Romans 5:8

But God shows his love for us in that while we were still
sinners, Christ died for us.

28. Romans 6:11

So you also must consider yourselves dead to sin and alive
to God in Christ Jesus.

29. Romans 6:23

For the wages of sin is death, but the free gift of God is
eternal life in Christ Jesus our Lord.

30. Romans 8:1

There is therefore now no condemnation for those who
are in Christ Jesus.

31. Romans 8:28

And we know that for those who love God all things work
together for good, for those who are called according to
his purpose.

32. Romans 12:1-2

I appeal to you therefore, brothers, by the mercies of
God, to present your bodies as a living sacrifice, holy and
acceptable to God, which is your spiritual worship. Do

not be conformed to this world but be transformed by the renewal of your mind, that by testing you may discern what is the will of God, what is good and acceptable and perfect.

33. 1 Corinthians 2:2

For I decided to know nothing among you except Jesus Christ and him crucified.

34. 1 Corinthians 10:13

No temptation has overtaken you that is not common to man. God is faithful, and he will not let you be tempted beyond your ability, but with the temptation he will also provide the way of escape, that you may be able to endure it.

35. 2 Corinthians 5:17

Therefore, if anyone is in Christ, he is a new creation. The old has passed away; behold, the new has come.

36. 2 Corinthians 5:21

For our sake he made him to be sin who knew no sin, so that in him we might become the righteousness of God.

37. Galatians 2:20

I have been crucified with Christ. It is no longer I who live, but Christ who lives in me. And the life I now live in the flesh I live by faith in the Son of God, who loved me and gave himself for me.

38. Galatians 5:1

For freedom Christ has set us free; stand firm therefore, and do not submit again to a yoke of slavery.

39. Galatians 5:22-23

But the fruit of the Spirit is love, joy, peace, patience, kindness, goodness, faithfulness, gentleness, self-control; against such things there is no law.

40. Ephesians 2:8-9

For by grace you have been saved through faith. And this is not your own doing; it is the gift of God, not a result of works, so that no one may boast.

41. Philippians 1:21

For to me to live is Christ, and to die is gain.

42. Philippians 4:6-7

Do not be anxious about anything, but in everything by prayer and supplication with thanksgiving let your requests be made known to God. And the peace of God, which surpasses all understanding, will guard your hearts and your minds in Christ Jesus.

43. 1 Thessalonians 5:16-18

Rejoice always, pray without ceasing, give thanks in all

circumstances; for this is the will of God in Christ Jesus for you.

44. 2 Timothy 1:7

For God gave us a spirit not of fear but of power and love and self-control.

45. 2 Timothy 3:16-17

All Scripture is breathed out by God and profitable for teaching, for reproof, for correction, and for training in righteousness, that the man of God may be complete, equipped for every good work.

46. Hebrews 11:6

And without faith it is impossible to please him, for whoever would draw near to God must believe that he exists and that he rewards those who seek him.

47. Hebrews 12:1-2

Therefore, since we are surrounded by so great a cloud of witnesses, let us also lay aside every weight, and sin which clings so closely, and let us run with endurance the race that is set before us, looking to Jesus, the founder and perfecter of our faith, who for the joy that was set before him endured the cross, despising the shame, and is seated at the right hand of the throne of God.

48. James 1:2-3

Count it all joy, my brothers, when you meet trials of various kinds, for you know that the testing of your faith produces steadfastness.

49. James 1:5

If any of you lacks wisdom, let him ask God, who gives generously to all without reproach, and it will be given him.

50. 1 John 1:9

If we confess our sins, he is faithful and just to forgive us our sins and to cleanse us from all unrighteousness.

51. 1 John 4:10

In this is love, not that we have loved God but that he loved us and sent his Son to be the propitiation for our sins.

52. Rev 1:5b-6

To him who loves us and has freed us from our sins by his blood and made us a kingdom, priests to his God and Father, to him be glory and dominion forever and ever. Amen.

Let me conclude with this anecdote told by Carolyn Weber in her marvelous book, *Surprised by Oxford:*

On my way to the lecture, I practiced reciting from Milton's *Paradise Lost* as I strode Longwall Street (British pragmatism embedded even in their infrastructure, given that the old road literally ran the length of a long wall). For our assignment next week, among other expectations, Dr. Nuttham required that we memorize several lines from the epic poem.

"What?" we all gasped in unison.

"Consider how easy you have it," he replied. "Many of the Romantics knew much of Milton by heart – how can you study these writers if you do not know what was in their hearts as they themselves wrote?" Then he added, thoughtfully, "While you are at it, I also suggest that you memorize the first few chapters of Genesis. So you know what was in Milton's heart too."

"Why memorize it? Why not just read it carefully?" argued Susan, our Yale graduate.

"Because what you memorize by heart, you take to heart," replied Dr. Nuttham simply. "It shouldn't be called by 'rote' but by 'root,' for you get at the source of the text, its foundation. Once you really absorb the words, the words become your own. Then, and only then, can you

mull them over on your tongue, appreciating
them as you would good wine, enjoying them
as the company of a good friend. Besides," he
added, "we always value something for which
we've had to labor." (p. 224)

When you learn God's words, they become your own.

Memorize God's Word. Hide it in your heart! Do it with a
partner, do it as a family, or do it by yourself, but get started
memorizing Scripture.

PART IV

RESPONSE TO COMMON
QUESTIONS & ISSUES

Chapter Eleven

QUESTIONS AND ISSUES

There is no explicit command in the Bible telling us to have a daily time alone with God. What about this?

That's true. There is no explicit command in those words. But there are many, many passages telling us to do the things that are part of this time with God – pray, give thanks, sing, read the Bible, seek the Lord, hear God's voice, give praise, confess your sin, and more.

Also, it is interesting that God does not spell out some things in the Bible as clearly as we would like, but yet for those who have an open heart, who have ears to hear, the truth is clearly taught. For example, the word Trinity is not found in the Bible. There is no succinct paragraph spelling out the nature of the Trinity and warning us against heresies. Yet for those open to God, the truth of the Trinity is clearly taught throughout the Bible.

Or take church attendance. Is weekly church attendance clearly commanded in the Bible? No it's not. There is the analogy of the Jewish Sabbath. There is the custom of Jesus with the synagogues. There is the challenge of Hebrews 10:24-25 which gets close but does not quite get there: "And let us consider how to stir up one another to love and good works, not neglecting to meet together, as is the habit of some, but encouraging one another, and all the more as you see the Day drawing near." There is the practice of the early church in Acts. But there is no clear, unequivocal command. Yet we don't need that. The truth is clearly taught in the Bible. We are called to meet together and encourage one another in our faith regularly, whether that's at a large mega-church or in a home church, or something in between.

Other examples could be given. The truths of the Bible are plain enough, if we have a humble heart ready to obey.

I find the reasons to meet alone with God overwhelming: I long to meet with him, God longs for it, I want to know and love God more, I need this daily time. Moreover, there is the repeated, strong emphasis in the Bible on the importance of prayer and the importance of the Bible.

This daily time with God may not be explicitly taught, but it is implicitly taught. It is clear enough for those with ears to hear.

Life is so busy today. Is daily unhurried time with God realistic for most people?

There's a lot to say about this one. This is the most common problem – or at least people think it is.

But there is a deeper issue – the issue of priorities, the issue of what's really important to us. Do we or do we not long for God? Do we thirst for him as a deer pants for water in the desert? Is his Word more valuable to me than all the billions of a Bill Gates or a Warren Buffett? When I meet with him, will the God of the universe, the living and holy and sovereign God, the God who created billions of galaxies with his mere breath, the God who loves us tenderly and fiercely and sent his own beloved Son to die for our sin on a bloody cross, will this God show up and meet with me and draw close to me? Will God be right there with me?

If we believe he will, if we believe the Bible is true and God will do what he says, then this is no issue at all. Too busy? For God? Are you kidding?

Forget the television! Forget the phones and social media! Forget all the trivialities of life! God is here! If we are too busy to meet with God, then we're busier than God wants us to be. The issue is not busyness, but priorities.

I dare say if the President of the United States showed up at your door or your office and asked for a half-hour with you, you would make time for him. Well, there's someone here greater than a President! For the U.S. President is a mere grasshopper compared to the Lord of glory! He is a mere man, whose breath is in his nostrils, here today and gone tomorrow.

We all make time for what we really want to do. Shallow people say: "I'm too busy. I don't have time for that." Honest people say: "I choose not to give time to that. I choose to put my time elsewhere."

Yes, in today's world we can be busy. There are so many options. There's not only the option of TV, but the option of 300 channels on TV! There's not just the option of a smart phone, but 500 million apps for the smart phone. There's not just one restaurant in the city, but hundreds of restaurants in the city. We have so much option.

But nothing has really changed. We each choose what's important to us. A mere mortal has the priceless privilege of meeting alone with the Almighty God. If I do anything, let me do this! Let me start here. After that, and only after that, then we will see what else we get to.

Jesus told us: "But seek first the kingdom of God and his righteousness, and all these things will be added to you" (Matthew 6:33).

Is a daily time with God legalistic? Should we not just meet with God, for prayer and Bible reading, whenever we want to?

Several thoughts. First of all, some people want to meet with God every day. It becomes delight, not duty or drudgery. But secondly, even if we meet with God out of discipline, that's not legalism. It would be legalism if we thought we were earning God's favor or approval. That's different than discipline.

Discipline says: "I will show up every day to meet with God, whether or not I feel like it, because I want to draw close to God and grow in Christ. Because God wants this time with me. Because I need it."

In Daniel 6:10 we see that Daniel got down on his knees three times a day to meet with God in prayer. That was discipline, not legalism.

Legalism reflects religion not the gospel. Religion does things for God in order to earn God's love and acceptance. The gospel does things for God because we have God's love and acceptance.

I pray throughout the day rather than in a special quiet time each day. Isn't this sufficient?

It's both/and not either/or. Yes we want to "pray without ceasing" (1 Thessalonians 5:17) and live continually in

God's presence. In some ways, the entire day should be one giant quiet time, one giant time with the Lord. We want to be in an attitude of prayer throughout the day, an attitude of dependence upon God, an attitude of listening to God's promptings. Often during the day this attitude will take voice and we will talk with the Lord.

But this doesn't preclude the need for a special time alone with the Lord. Jesus lived in prayer and yet had special focused times of prayer. Daniel did both. I'm sure David did both. And Paul. And other godly people in the Bible.

And then in history and in life today, all of God's intimates had both an attitude of prayer and a special time with God in the secret. An unhurried time. A time alone in the secret place.

Besides, prayer throughout the day doesn't include time in God's Word, which is of utmost importance.

Richard Foster, who wrote the powerful books Celebration of Discipline and Prayer, argued that we should never excuse our prayerlessness under the guise of praying throughout the day. He then relays this quote: "The truth is that we only learn to pray all the time everywhere after we have resolutely set about praying some of the time somewhere." (Prayer, 74)

This question is a non-issue, unless you are looking for an

excuse to not meet with God. Let me remind you: You are not doing God a favor to meet alone with him. He's doing you a favor. An amazing favor. This is not duty; it's privilege. The highest privilege granted to a mere human.

It seems that some people have a quiet time for years and yet they never change or grow. What's wrong?

That can certainly happen. In the same way innumerable Christians go to Christ-honoring churches for years and yet show little or no growth in Christlikeness.

A person can have a quiet time and never connect with God. We can go through the motions to check a box. We can focus on knowledge about God rather than knowledge of God. We can come to God with just our head rather than our heart and our head. We can become spiritually proud and self-righteous.

We will not grow in Christ's love just because we clock time alone with God. But if we show up with a humble heart because we want to meet God and seek his face and call out to him, then God in his mercy will meet with us and transform us. The transformation may not happen as quickly as we'd like, but over a long time, over months and years, God will make us more like Jesus.

———

This book has put all the emphasis on meeting with God alone. But isn't it vital to pray and study Scripture with other believers?

Absolutely, it is! Praying and studying the Bible with others is vital. But that's not the purpose of this book.

So many of the prayers in the Psalms, so many of the prayers throughout the Bible, are prayed in public not in private. Even the Lord's Prayer reflects the setting of community: "Our Father … Give us this day."

When it comes to prayer and Bible reading, we need time alone and we need time together. Again, it's both/and not either/or.

However, if we are always with people then it is likely that we will not have anything to bring to people when we are with them. But if we meet God in the secret place, then God will pour into us, and he will use us to bring his love and truth and wisdom and grace to the people we encounter. Otherwise, we will be people with empty hearts and hollow chests.

———

Will a daily quiet time foster spiritual pride?

It certainly could. Spiritual pride, the worst form of pride, is a real possibility and it must be vigilantly guarded against. If you meet with God alone each day, and you know other believers do not take this regular time in prayer and the Bible, pretty soon you might think you're more spiritual than others. You might congratulate yourself on your heart for God and end up farther from Christ not closer to Christ.

This is a danger – and a deadly one! But the solution is not to stop meeting with God for prayer and Bible reading! No! That's Satan's solution for you. God's solution is that you humble yourself like a little child and come to him in brokenness and humility. God's solution is that you stop comparing yourself with anyone else, but simply focus on your own need to seek God's face. God's solution is that you come to God like the tax collector in Luke 18, who cried out "God, be merciful to me, a sinner!" – and not like the Pharisee who congratulated himself for being so spiritual.

Be aware of this danger. Be aware that knowledge puffs up or makes arrogant (1 Corinthians 8:1). Remind yourself that your goal is not knowledge about God but knowledge of God, God himself. You want God, not information. Come to God for your heart and not just for your head. Don't simply read through the Bible. Pray through the Bible. "Lord, speak to me. Change me. Lord, I'm desperate for you."

In Isaiah 66:2 there is a powerful challenge:

> All these things my hand has made,
>   and so all these things came to be,
>   declares the Lord.

But this is the one to whom I will look:
he who is humble and contrite in spirit
and trembles at my word.

God is looking for men and women who are humble, who are contrite in spirit, and who tremble at God's Word. Be such a person! By God's grace, be such a person.

Chapter Twelve

EPILOGUE

———————

Dear reader, this is my prayer for you: That you would meet with God, alone, each day, to draw close to him, to love and be loved. And that this would become the delight of your life. That's also my prayer for me.

Decide that this time in the secret will be part of your life. Pre-decide. Decide what, if anything, you need to give up or change. Ask the Lord. Choose a default time and place – say, in my living room early, after breakfast, for about a half hour, before anyone else is there.

Then, show up. Tell him you love him and want to love him more. Intentionally enter into his presence. Praise him, thank him. Perhaps sing quietly to him. Ask him to speak to you. Listen. Ask him if there's anything you need to hear today. If you sense God putting something on your heart, write it in a notepad. Open your Bible, say to Matthew 1. Read a chapter a day, or maybe just a paragraph. Ask God to speak to you through Scripture. Talk with him as you read. Ask him to change you. Then pray simple, heartfelt prayers for yourself and others. God loves it when you depend upon him for all your needs. God loves it when you intercede for others.

Then, do it again tomorrow. And the next day. And every day after that. For the rest of your life.

Meet with God. Alone. Unhurried. In the secret. Draw close. Receive his love. Love him back. Call out. Listen. Adore. Be caught up in wonder, love and praise.

"O begin! It is for your life!"

Appendix

Bible Memory

1. **Joshua 1:8**

   This Book of the Law shall not depart from your mouth, but you shall meditate on it day and night, so that you may be careful to do according to all that is written in it. For then you will make your way prosperous, and then you will have good success.

2. **Psalm 103:11-12**

   For as high as the heavens are above the earth,
       so great is his steadfast love toward those who fear him;
   as far as the east is from the west,
       so far does he remove our transgressions from us.

3. Proverbs 3:5-6

Trust in the LORD with all your heart,
    and do not lean on your own understanding
In all your ways acknowledge him,
    and he will make straight your paths.

4. Isaiah 53:6

All we like sheep have gone astray;
    we have turned—every one—to his own way;
and the LORD has laid on him
    the iniquity of us all.

5. Jeremiah 9:23-24

Thus says the LORD: "Let not the wise man boast in his wisdom, let not the mighty man boast in his might, let not the rich man boast in his riches, but let him who boasts boast in this, that he understands and knows me, that I am the LORD who practices steadfast love, justice, and righteousness in the earth. For in these things I delight, declares the LORD."

6. Matthew 4:19

And he said to them, "Follow me, and I will make you fishers of men."

7. Matthew 11:28

Come to me, all who labor and are heavy laden, and I will give you rest.

8. **Matthew 22:37-39**

   And he said to him, "You shall love the Lord your God with all your heart and with all your soul and with all your mind. This is the great and first commandment. And a second is like it: You shall love your neighbor as yourself."

9. **Matthew 23:12**

   Whoever exalts himself will be humbled, and whoever humbles himself will be exalted.

10. **Matthew 28:18-20**

    And Jesus came and said to them, "All authority in heaven and on earth has been given to me. Go therefore and make disciples of all nations, baptizing them in the name of the Father and of the Son and of the Holy Spirit, teaching them to observe all that I have commanded you. And behold, I am with you always, to the end of the age."

11. **Mark 10:45**

    For even the Son of Man came not to be served but to serve, and to give his life as a ransom for many.

12. **Luke 9:23**

    And he said to all, "If anyone would come after me, let him deny himself and take up his cross daily and follow me."

13. **John 1:1**

    In the beginning was the Word, and the Word was with God, and the Word was God.

14. John 1:12

But to all who did receive him, who believed in his name, he gave the right to become children of God.

15. John 1:14

And the Word became flesh and dwelt among us, and we have seen his glory, glory as of the only Son from the Father, full of grace and truth.

16. John 3:16

For God so loved the world, that he gave his only Son, that whoever believes in him should not perish but have eternal life.

17. John 8:31-32

So Jesus said to the Jews who had believed him, "If you abide in my word, you are truly my disciples, and you will know the truth, and the truth will set you free."

18. John 13:35

By this all people will know that you are my disciples, if you have love for one another.

19. John 14:1

Let not your hearts be troubled. Believe in God; believe also in me.

20. John 14:6

Jesus said to him, "I am the way, and the truth, and the life. No one comes to the Father except through me."

21. John 14:21

Whoever has my commandments and keeps them, he it is who loves me. And he who loves me will be loved by my Father, and I will love him and manifest myself to him.

22. Acts 1:8

But you will receive power when the Holy Spirit has come upon you, and you will be my witnesses in Jerusalem and in all Judea and Samaria, and to the end of the earth.

23. Acts 16:31

And they said, "Believe in the Lord Jesus, and you will be saved, you and your household."

24. Romans 1:16

For I am not ashamed of the gospel, for it is the power of God for salvation to everyone who believes, to the Jew first and also to the Greek.

25. Romans 3:23

For all have sinned and fall short of the glory of God.

26. Romans 3:25-26

Whom God put forward as a propitiation by his blood, to be received by faith. This was to show God's righteousness, because in his divine forbearance he had passed over former sins. It was to show his righteousness at the present time, so that he might be just and the justifier of the one who has faith in Jesus.

27. Romans 5:8

But God shows his love for us in that while we were still sinners, Christ died for us.

28. Romans 6:11

So you also must consider yourselves dead to sin and alive to God in Christ Jesus.

29. Romans 6:23

For the wages of sin is death, but the free gift of God is eternal life in Christ Jesus our Lord.

30. Romans 8:1

There is therefore now no condemnation for those who are in Christ Jesus.

31. Romans 8:28

And we know that for those who love God all things work together for good, for those who are called according to his purpose.

32. Romans 12:1-2

I appeal to you therefore, brothers, by the mercies of God, to present your bodies as a living sacrifice, holy and acceptable to God, which is your spiritual worship. Do not be conformed to this world but be transformed by the renewal of your mind, that by testing you may discern what is the will of God, what is good and acceptable and perfect.

33. 1 Corinthians 2:2

For I decided to know nothing among you except Jesus Christ and him crucified.

34. 1 Corinthians 10:13

No temptation has overtaken you that is not common to man. God is faithful, and he will not let you be tempted beyond your ability, but with the temptation he will also provide the way of escape, that you may be able to endure it.

35. 2 Corinthians 5:17

Therefore, if anyone is in Christ, he is a new creation. The old has passed away; behold, the new has come.

36. 2 Corinthians 5:21

For our sake he made him to be sin who knew no sin, so that in him we might become the righteousness of God.

37. Galatians 2:20

I have been crucified with Christ. It is no longer I who live, but Christ who lives in me. And the life I now live in the flesh I live by faith in the Son of God, who loved me and gave himself for me.

38. Galatians 5:1

For freedom Christ has set us free; stand firm therefore, and do not submit again to a yoke of slavery.

39. Galatians 5:22-23

But the fruit of the Spirit is love, joy, peace, patience, kindness, goodness, faithfulness, gentleness, self-control; against such things there is no law.

40. Ephesians 2:8-9

For by grace you have been saved through faith. And this is not your own doing; it is the gift of God, not a result of works, so that no one may boast.

41. Philippians 1:21

For to me to live is Christ, and to die is gain.

42. Philippians 4:6-7

Do not be anxious about anything, but in everything by prayer and supplication with thanksgiving let your requests be made known to God. And the peace of God, which surpasses all understanding, will guard your hearts and your minds in Christ Jesus.

43. 1 Thessalonians 5:16-18

Rejoice always, pray without ceasing, give thanks in all circumstances; for this is the will of God in Christ Jesus for you.

44. 2 Timothy 1:7

For God gave us a spirit not of fear but of power and love and self-control.

45. 2 Timothy 3:16-17

All Scripture is breathed out by God and profitable for teaching, for reproof, for correction, and for training in righteousness, that the man of God may be complete, equipped for every good work.

46. Hebrews 11:6

And without faith it is impossible to please him, for whoever would draw near to God must believe that he exists and that he rewards those who seek him.

47. Hebrews 12:1-2

Therefore, since we are surrounded by so great a cloud of witnesses, let us also lay aside every weight, and sin which clings so closely, and let us run with endurance the race that is set before us, looking to Jesus, the founder and perfecter of our faith, who for the joy that was set before him endured the cross, despising the shame, and is seated at the right hand of the throne of God.

48. James 1:2-3

Count it all joy, my brothers, when you meet trials of various kinds, for you know that the testing of your faith produces steadfastness.

49. James 1:5

If any of you lacks wisdom, let him ask God, who gives generously to all without reproach, and it will be given him.

50. 1 John 1:9

If we confess our sins, he is faithful and just to forgive us our sins and to cleanse us from all unrighteousness.

51. 1 John 4:10

In this is love, not that we have loved God but that he loved us and sent his Son to be the propitiation for our sins.

52. Rev 1:5b-6

To him who loves us and has freed us from our sins by his blood and made us a kingdom, priests to his God and Father, to him be glory and dominion forever and ever. Amen.

ABOUT THE AUTHOR

Jeff, the founding Pastor at WoodsEdge Community Church, grew up in Madisonville, Texas. He became a believer in the summer before attending Rice University where he majored in History and was a four-time All-American recipient in track and cross country. While at Rice, he also received the Bob Quin Award as Outstanding Student Athlete.

Jeff is a graduate of Dallas Theological Seminary where he earned the Master of Theology and Doctor of Ministry degrees. Jeff and his wife Gayle met in Oregon where Jeff was serving in a church internship and running for Nike. When they met, Gayle was working as a nurse.

Also By Jeff Wells

The Great Verses:
365 Verses to Learn, to Love, To Live

A compilation of 365 great verses from the Bible paired with a meaningful devotional for each.

Breaking Free from OCD

An autobiographical account of Jeff's intense struggle with Obsessive-Compulsive Disorder during his adult years and how he overcame it.

LOVE: Revealing the Heart of God

A coffee table book that combines artistic elements with inspirational daily devotionals focused on the love of God.

www.jeffhwells.com